PRAISE FOR *ASTROLOGY BY MOONLIGHT*

"*Astrology by Moonlight* proves today's astrology can be penetratingly accurate, widely accessible, and filled with genuine wisdom. The root power of the book derives from a comprehensive and cross-cultural explanation of the astrological Moon on which any astrologer or astrolyte would be foolish not to take notes. This deep analysis is then impressively applied to the Moon's phases with each planet. This is truly a book for our times in that it addresses each of us as complex embodiments of the flow of consciousness rather than as products of a frozen birth chart."

—Adam Gainsburg, founder of Soulsign Astrology

"Tara Aal and Aswin Subramanyan meld the principles of Western evolutionary astrology and the centrality of the Moon in Jyotish, the Hindu system of astrology, to produce a fresh understanding of lunar symbolism in personal development … The result is a novel and thought-provoking treatise that expands our understanding of the role of the Moon as a symbol in human psychology and astrological predictive work. East truly meets West in this volume, and it is well worth reading and contemplation."

—Anthony Louis, author of *Horary Astrology*

"This thorough and thought-provoking book is a powerful collaboration between two astrologers who come from different astrological traditions yet create a synergy and resonance that opens doors to both the heart and the mind. Get ready to explore new territory by joining these two fine astrologers as they traverse the rich undercurrents that exist when you delve into how each planet connects to the Moon through the phases. Not only will it expand your astrological knowledge, it will expand your awareness."

astro

© Y. Niveditha

ABOUT ASWIN SUBRAMANYAN

Aswin Subramanyan, an astrologer from India, has a foundation in Vedic astrology, but he developed a keen interest in Hellenistic and medieval astrology, and his practice is a blend of all three traditional forms. He was equally impressed by the psychological and evolutionary-oriented approach of the evolutionary astrologers. Aswin is extremely focused on bridging the gap between the Eastern and medieval Persian/European forms of astrology. His book on the Persian time-lord technique, *Firdaria: Periods of Life,* was published in March 2021. He is currently writing his next book about annual predictive methods, which will bring together the works of the Greeks, Persians and Indians and provide a practical framework to use these works in practice.

In addition to being an astrologer, writer, and publisher, Aswin works in an investment bank. He has a double master's degree in Finance and Labour Management and is interested in the global economy and finance. When not practicing astrology, Aswin enjoys playing south Indian classical music on his electric guitar. He is also a perennial student of Vedantic philosophy and Greek philosophy. He believes that the way of life was written years ago, and we just have different lenses to view the same thing in different ways at different times. Aswin's philosophy towards life is to live and let live! To know more, you can always get in touch by visiting www.theabverdict.com.

© Darren Morales

ABOUT TARA AAL

Tara Aal is an evolutionary astrologer, writer, artist, and tarot reader. In addition to writing *Astrology by Moonlight*, she is co-author of *Natural Astrology: Houses, Signs, Planets*. Tara's approach to the archetypes is experiential and creative, including the astrological technique Planets on the 1st. She created a series of YouTube videos titled "We Are the Planets" through Evolutionary Astrology (EA) Zoom Meetings. Tara studied extensively with Laura Nalbandian and Adam Gainsburg (Soulsign Astrology).

Since 2010, Tara has been building her practice through clients, teaching, art, and writing. Her speaking engagements include Northwest Astrological Conference (NORWAC), United Astrology Conference (UAC), Kepler College, Washington State Astrological Association, International Society for Astrological Research (ISAR), Astrology of Awakening Summits, and the Indian Institute of Oriental Heritage. Tara's work has appeared in many publications, including *The Mountain Astrologer* and *Infinity Astrological Magazine*. She's currently the resident astrologer and lead writer for *Sage Goddess* and serves on the International Society for Astrological Research Board as marketing director. Tara is also passionate about music, photography, painting, drawing, and exploring nature and the outdoors. You can learn more and reach her at www.TaraAal.com.

ASTROLOGY BY MOONLIGHT

ASTROLOGY BY MOONLIGHT

Exploring the Relationship Between Moon Phases & Planets to Improve & Illuminate Your Life

TARA AAL

ASWIN SUBRAMANYAN

LLEWELLYN PUBLICATIONS
WOODBURY, MINNESOTA

First Edition
First Printing, 2021

Book design by Samantha Peterson
Cover design by Kevin R. Brown
Photo provided by the authors

Library of Congress Cataloging-in-Publication Data
Names: Aal, Tara, author. | Subramanyan, Aswin, author.
Title: Astrology by moonlight : exploring the relationship between moon phases & planets to improve & illuminate your life / Tara Aal, Aswin Subramanyan.
Description: First edition. | Woodbury, MN : Llewellyn Publications, [2021] | Includes bibliographical references.
Identifiers: LCCN 2021039634 (print) | LCCN 2021039635 (ebook) | ISBN 9780738768717 (paperback) | ISBN 9780738769790 (ebook)
Subjects: LCSH: Moon—Phases—Miscellanea. | Astrology.
Classification: LCC BF1623.M66 A325 2021 (print) | LCC BF1623.M66 (ebook) | DDC 133.5/3—dc23
LC record available at https://lccn.loc.gov/2021039634
LC ebook record available at https://lccn.loc.gov/2021039635

Llewellyn Publications
A Division of Llewellyn Worldwide Ltd.
2143 Wooddale Drive
Woodbury, MN 55125-2989
www.llewellyn.com
Printed in the United States of America

OTHER BOOKS BY ASWIN SUBRAMANYAN

Firdaria: Periods of Life

OTHER BOOKS BY TARA AAL

Natural Astrology: Houses, Signs, Planets

DEDICATION

We dedicate this book to you, the reader, and to the collective consciousness. All creations, no matter how personal they may seem or feel, are the result of our interconnectivity. Thank you to each and every part of Us.

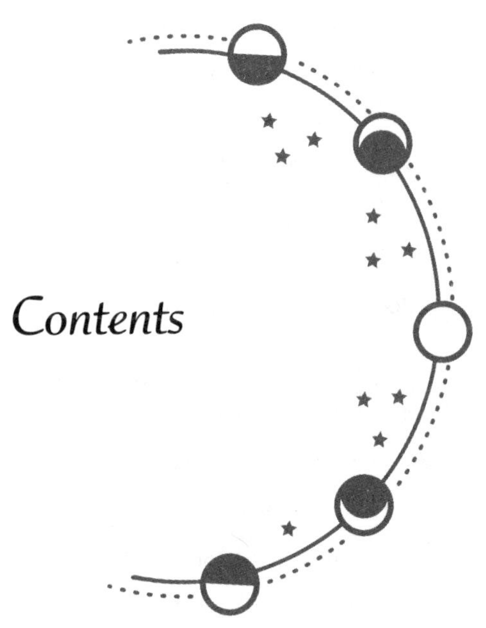

Contents

Acknowledgments

FROM ASWIN SUBRAMANYAN

Hailing from a family of astrologers whose lineage goes back at least 250 years, it would be safe to say that astrology in me is basically due to "great genes." I didn't find astrology, but astrology found its way inside me through my maternal blood as most of my maternal family members are exposed to some form of astrology and divination. With a foundation in Vedic astrology, I also took a keen interest in Hellenistic and medieval astrologies. Evolutionary astrology rang the bell in my brain through Steven Forrest's *The Inner Sky* and other wonderful lectures on the Facebook forum Evolutionary Astrology (EA) Zoom Meetings. The psychological insights and soulful talks in some meetings inspired me, and this was one of the forums where I was introduced to the work of my dear friend, Tara Aal. I'm eternally grateful to Tara for having faith in me. I am so glad I found her work through the wonderful *Infinity Astrological Magazine* published by Smiljana Gavrančić. And although I had known Tara's writings (especially regarding tarot) at least a year before I contacted her, I never realized we'd write a book together.

Tara's pure heart and genuineness made me feel extremely comfortable to remain myself, which is one of the strongest reasons for our successful bonding. Without love and mutual respect, we wouldn't have completed this book. Although this is not an enormous book, it was certainly not as easy to write as we expected it to be. We faced some personal challenges that stalled our work, but we came back strong to complete the book at one stretch. It looks like we were destined to come together. The three days Tara and I spent in New Delhi together along with her partner, Darren, and my family clearly defined my path for the next few years of my life, and I am extremely grateful for our friendship.

Thanks to Robert Wilkinson for having multiple spiritually inclined conversations with me. Reviewing them makes so much sense and they have deep meaning, which helps me understand some of the hardcore realities of life. Michelle Young is solely responsible for who I am in the community today. She has been a kind master, and I owe her a majority of credit for me being a writer today. Since 2018, only I know how much my writing has improved because of Michelle and I'm extremely thankful to her.

When I look back at my life as an astrologer over thirty years, the void would have been incomplete without Lars Panaro and Rok Koritnik. These are my buddies and my brothers with whom I learned and explored the deepest and widest horizons of traditional astrology of both the East and the West. Endless conversations at odd hours of the day and night shaped me as an astrologer, and I'm deeply grateful for my paths having crossed with theirs.

Thanks to Tania Daniels for the positive impact she has had in my astrological studies, and I value her friendship very much. I admire her generosity and straightforward attitude. She probably doesn't know that I took the conversation with her as a motivation to apply to be a speaker at the Astrology Association (AA) conference 2020 in London. Tania is like an elder sister to me and I am very glad our paths crossed.

Sharon Knight, apart from being a pleasant human being, is a very generous person. I have learned things about astrology from many people, but I learned how to be a responsible astrologer from Sharon. What makes her a consummate astrologer of our times is her generosity in helping the next generation of talented astrologers grow, which develops the entire community. She always sees the bigger picture and that's a huge learning for me.

Anthony Louis taught me primary directions completely and so much more. Every conversation I have with him is absolutely engaging and fantastic, and each is a significant learning experience. I have never had these types of conversations with anyone else because I never had an actual teacher in astrology. I owe my deepest gratitude to him.

Thanks to Martin Gansten, Frank Clifford, Chris Brennan, Benjamin Dykes, P James Clark, Gary Lorentzen, Kieron Devlin, Steve Wolfson, Linda Johnson (EA Zoom Meetings) and Nadia Mierau for inspiring me in many different ways.

I seek the blessings of my mentor, Mr. Gurumurthy Iyer (my maternal grandfather), who inspired me to take up astrology. Learning from a person who has been into astrology for about sixty years is the greatest gift to a millennial like me, and I hope I don't fail to hold on to the opportunity. Although I cannot match his genius, I hope I can keep the tradition going and carry on the legacy by following in his footprints and passing on the beacon to the next generation.

I wish my father was alive to see this day. He is my only icon and role model in life, and I'm thankful that I had this opportunity of human experience alongside him as a son. I am grateful to my mother, B Buvaneswari, who selflessly stands behind the family to make sure everyone remains happy, especially after my father's sudden and untimely demise in 2013. My twin sisters, Nandhini Subramanyan and Ranjani Subramanyan, have been an inseparable part of my life since their birth. We have never thanked each other in anything because things are so easy and informal between the three of us. Last but not least, my wife, Niveditha, and my son, Guru, thank you for adding more meaning and value to my life.

FROM TARA AAL

For the past decade, I've been exploring how to work with astrology in ways that feel true to me and make the best use of my strengths and gifts. I don't expect that exploration to ever end, but this book and my collaboration with Aswin in creating it have hit home. It wasn't always easy; in fact, both Aswin and I experienced a few months of fatigue and lingering illness—at the same time across the world from each other! We had to take a break, even if it meant we'd miss our initial publishing deadline that he had determined by electional astrology. At that time, both feeling a little discouraged and ragged, we said, "What would the Moon say?" And the answer was, of course, to take care of ourselves and rest. Like good moonchildren, we listened and took that advice. That break and time away from the computer screen were so important. I can't imagine having written the rest of the book (Uranus, Neptune, and Pluto in particular) without a personal shift in consciousness. That shift came through a phase of relaxing, reading, and learning, and what I can best call re-wiring. I am better for it and so is the book!

Thank you, Aswin, for finding me in the astrological community and suggesting we write this book. It's been synchronistic and serendipitous ever since. I admire your initiative, insight, determination, and generous spirit. It's an honor to co-create with you and to be your friend.

My heartfelt gratitude to all my teachers, clients, and students. Special thanks to Laura Nalbandian and Adam Gainsburg whose wisdom, guidance, support, and example have greatly helped shape my practice of astrology and my evolution as a human being. Thank you to Dane Rudhyar, Jeffrey Wolf Green, Steven Forrest, Mark Jones, Liz Greene, Howard Sasportas, Stephen Arroyo, Walter Jager, Jason Holley, Linda Jonson and EA Zoom Meetings, Smiljana Gavrančić and Infinity Astrological Magazine, Sue Rose Minahan and Talk Cosmos, Lisa Wallace (Raven Bella Zingaro), Christina Caudill and Radiant Astrology, Lesley Francis, and Jiddu Krishnamurti. Your work, presence, and contributions have influenced, inspired, and grown me. Thank you to Tess Sterling for seeing my potential and putting me to work at the beginning of my metaphysical career, and to the Stargazers Bookstore community for continued love and support. Thank you, Athena Perrakis, Dave Meizlik, Claire Gutschow, and my work family at Sage Goddess for support and so many opportunities to learn, grow, and share. And to Christopher Laubenthal, who gifted me my first astrology book in unsuspecting circumstances, thank you for sparking up this part of me and feeding those flames.

I'm so grateful for my loving family: my biological family, and that of my partner, Darren, and my bonus (step) daughter. I've been blessed with so much stability, care, and kindness. I love each one of you.

Thank you, Darren Morales, for a life, home, and heart filled with love. You push me to my edge and somehow are also my soft landing. Being a "we" with you makes me a better me. Thank you for seeing and loving me as I am and staying through it all.

To everyone who's been a part of my life, thank you. To all of you with whom I've had those intimate, vulnerable, life-changing conversations and shared in magical moments, huge thank you. You know who you are and I'm grateful for you every day.

And finally, thank you to everyone reading this book, for taking this Moon journey with us. It's a joy to share it with you.

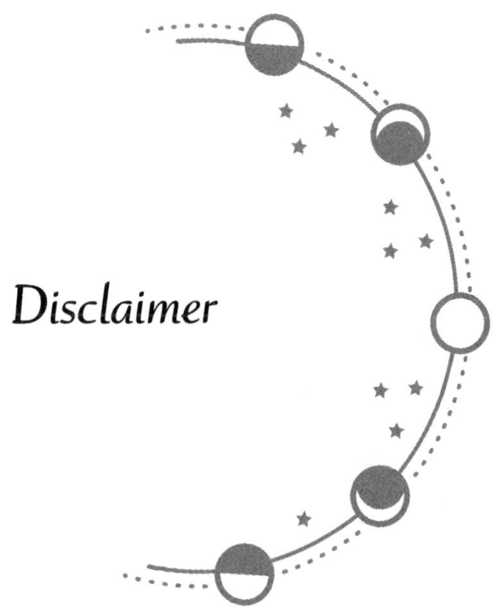

Disclaimer

This book is not intended to be a substitute for the advice of your personal physician or licensed mental health practitioner. For diagnosis and treatment of any physical or mental health condition, consult a licensed professional. The intent of the authors is to offer information of a general nature to support you in your quest for emotional, physical, and spiritual well-being. The publisher and author are not responsible for any condition that may require professional supervision and are not liable for any damages or negative consequences from any action by any person reading, following, or applying the information provided in this book.

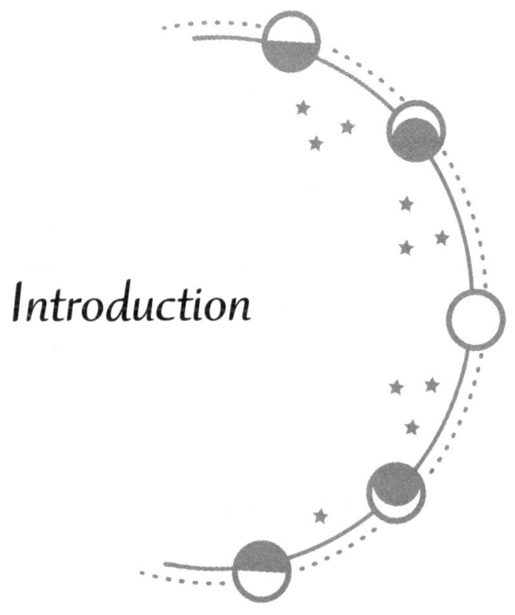

Introduction

We're all simultaneously living two lives—one inside ourselves and one in relationship to the external world. In this book, we work with the Moon as the most personal significator; the symbol of our most instinctual and primal human selves. The Moon in each of us is emotionally motivated and reactive. We all know that love, anger, jealousy, and despair can make us do seemingly crazy things. In some ways, when our emotions take over, we *are* out of our minds. Just feel that for a moment. Anytime we work with the Moon, it's so important to feel; there's really no other way to connect with this part of ourselves and each other. And when we want to be felt by someone, it's their Moon we unconsciously seek.

If Moon were a person, it's who we'd tell our troubles to. In daily life, as we know it, not everything and everyone cares about our troubles. We're all finding our way between that inner world and emotion that feels so real and what's going on in a broader context, where nothing, no matter how much it seems, is truly personal.

WORKING WITH THIS BOOK

This is a book about the Moon, and the Moon is associated with common everyday people, so it's for everyone. The Moon influences all of us, whether or not we pay any attention to astrology. The Moon is the closest astronomical body to Earth, and its gravity causes ocean tides and stabilizes our planet's axial tilt. Without the Moon, Earth would spin on its side, significantly changing our climate and seasons. In many ways, the Moon holds us in our current state of reality—not to mention it lights our nights and is our literal stepping stone to the rest of this universe. We know women's menstrual cycles naturally align with the moon cycle, and it's crazy to think the Moon doesn't affect us on other personal levels (ask anyone working in emergency rooms). Consider too the word *lunacy*, which means "moonstruck."

Astrology relates cosmic planetary movements to life on Earth and the inner and external lives of individuals. The Moon reflects our most personal, inner selves. It represents our emotional nature, habits, memory, moods, history, roots, sensations, reactions, and our need for comfort, security, and belonging. In the birth chart, the Moon by sign and house shows how you can best nurture yourself and others, what you need for emotional balance, and what makes your heart happy. It's a key to living a life of more ease and feeling good day-to-day.

Ultimately, this book is about the Moon in relationship to the other planets (your most personal self in relationship to other parts of you), but it also includes in-depth information about the

Moon and each of the planets, making it great for beginners. It also explains the eight soli-lunar phases, which we generally call moon phases. Moon phases are simply the physical relationship between the Moon and Sun in the sky; that is, how we see them come together for the new moon and oppose each other for the full moon. We can apply these phases to the relationship between any two bodies in the solar system—so you can use this book to learn about the basic moon phases and how to work with the Moon in its phases with other planets. You can then go beyond that and apply a phase to any planetary relationship you want.

Working with the Moon and moon phases is powerful because it helps you get more in touch with yourself and the cycles of nature. Nature has a rhythm, and so do you. Aligning to your personal rhythm and then syncing up with nature gets you in the flow. When you're in the flow, life is easier. What this really means is you get out of your own way and start working *with* the energy inside and out of you.

An easy way to start doing this is by paying attention to the current moon phase and getting the most out of that energy. For example, the new moon is the beginning of the moon cycle, so it's the best time to start new things and set new intentions. The end of the moon cycle, the balsamic phase, is a time to release and let the old wash away. From a practical standpoint, it's a great time to tweeze or wax your hair—it comes out easier. Then you can look at the moon phase you were born under. Consciously activating that energy helps you do almost everything better. You'll learn more about your natal moon phase in chapter 1, Planetary Cycles and Phases. Overall, understanding the Moon part of you and giving it what it needs is self-love that's not only good for your psychological well-being but also improves your daily material life. It all starts with you. If you want more you, go to the Moon!

This book doesn't go into Moon signs or houses, but there are many free online astrology resources. You can look up your moon sign and learn more about it at Cafeastrology.com/whats-my-moon-sign. This book does cover general moon phases, but you can find more information from the following resources: Tarot.com/astrology/moon-phases and Cafeastrology.com/calendars/moonphasescalendar.

Astrology is a language of energy and we all experience that energy, whether we know astrology or not. Those are just words and concepts to describe the energy. Anyone can read about cycles and phases and relate to the development of each stage. Even if you're new to astrology or don't know it at all, we hope you'll find value in the following chapters on the Moon in relationship to each of the traditional planets plus Pluto. There's substantial information about each planet and what it represents in us, so it's filled with astrological basics in addition to more intermediate phase exploration. We provide some basic instruction in chapter 1, but if you can't figure out how to calculate your personal planetary phases, it's a good excuse to ask an astrologer for help or learn a little more yourself. And don't forget these are just symbols. Your experience is your real teacher. If the reading and learning ever get in the way of that, take a break from it, including from this book.

A NOTE ABOUT ASTROLOGY IN HUMAN HISTORY

Astrology is arguably the greatest gift to mankind. When astrology started to fade towards the late seventeenth century, it took great efforts to bring it back to the forefront of mainstream human life. Although it didn't take its original form, some of the works of influential authors such as Dane Rudhyar, Marc Edmund Jones, and

Evangeline Adams changed the way people looked at astrology and started an understanding that astrology is much more than just the sun sign columns.

Dane Rudhyar's books *The Astrology of Personality* and *The Lunation Cycle* laid the foundation of what is today considered to be humanistic astrology, where archetypes play a major role in understanding the inner self of a human being. Carl Jung's book *Synchronicity* influenced later authors, including Richard Tarnas, who published a pathbreaking work with his book *Cosmos and Psyche*.

One common factor in most of the psychological forms of astrology is that they talk about the characteristic traits and nature of a human being; the way a human's psyche is being influenced or reflected by transits, progressions, and planetary cycles. So the idea of planetary cycles is as old as astrology itself if we look back to the ancient texts of Hellenistic Egypt, Persia, and India. However, our effort in understanding the nature and quality of life both internally and externally through the cycles of the Moon with respect to all the planets individually is a new and refreshing concept we couldn't refrain from writing about.

THE MAKING OF THIS BOOK

This book has been a divine calling and blessing. It's difficult to put into words, and so much of it seemed to happen almost on its own—except the writing itself! We recorded a Celestial Vibes podcast episode together on August 12, 2018—one day after a Leo New Moon Solar Eclipse—that went live on September 5, 2018. That podcast started this conversation about the Moon, heart, and mind, which led to writing a joint article about the Moon and Mercury, which eventually turned into this book. We were meant to work together, and when we met in person in March 2019 at the Indian Institute of Oriental Heritage International Astrological Conference in New Delhi, our fate was sealed. That trip transformed us into dear friends and right after that, this book arose to be written. And we could only say yes!

© Darren Morales, DarrenMorales.com

We practice different types of astrology—one of us Vedic with a predictive background, and the other Western, based in evolutionary astrology. One element that unites Vedic and evolutionary astrology is the belief in reincarnation, but this book isn't an attempt to compare or contrast our practices. It's our coming together to explore the cycles of nature and how they manifest in us, as human beings. Everything in this book is offered as a perspective or idea to investigate for yourself. We're both relatively young in our astrological careers and this material doesn't come from years and years of specific research, at least not in this lifetime. We wanted to apply our knowledge, insights, and experiences as practicing astrologers in a new way that would challenge us to grow and inspire others to think in different ways.

We chose the Moon as the focal point in this material because it represents the most personal aspect of ourselves in astrology. It's seen as the ego with its needs and attachments and as the heart of who we are that holds our memories, emotions, and humanity. Not a mere coincidence, the Moon is prominent in both of our natal charts. One of us was born with a Moon-Mars conjunction and the other a Moon-Jupiter conjunction—a perfect recipe for a Moon book! Before we settled on the title *Astrology by Moonlight*, we had considered the title *Releasing the Moon*, as a metaphor for how we're all releasing the light of our true spirit or essence. You'll see some references to "releasing the Moon" or "the Moon being released" throughout these pages. Just as the Moon reflects the light of the Sun, we are humans reflecting the light of our souls. Embracing the Moon is embracing our humanity—what we're all here to do. Writing this book has challenged us to think in new ways and unite our different perspectives and styles. In this East meets West collaboration, we found that the best meeting place is the heart, which is ironic for a book of words, but is nevertheless true.

ONE
Planetary Cycles and Phases

Energy overlaps and mixes; that is, we're always coming from something and moving toward something. And although we can learn about things selectively, focusing on their pure energy or essence, real life is often full of blending and contrasting. In endings we sense beginnings, and in beginnings we sense endings—neither exists without the other. The same is true of lightness and darkness. For what would the meaning of lightness be if there was no darkness? If there were no endings, what would become of beginnings?

This all applies to planetary synodic cycles, which are simply the changing relationship between two moving bodies. The word *synodic* relates to the conjunction between planets or any cosmic bodies. A synodic cycle begins at the conjunction and ends at the next conjunction.

In this book, we look at the synodic cycle of the Moon with each of the planets. We're all collectively and individually involved in many cycles, all happening at the same time. In the pages to follow, we look at a very small percentage of cycles. There's always so much more happening, influencing, alchemizing. As we often say, "Nothing happens in a vacuum." Nothing is truly separate.

Planetary cycles are very significant in mundane and natal astrology, giving an overall picture of what the specific relationship between two planets has to offer the world and its people. In modern days, many astrologers compellingly use planetary cycles in natal astrology to give their clients a clear idea of the specific phases of growth and development they're experiencing. It's common to analyze the relationship between Sun and Moon in a secondary progressed chart. Likewise, cycles of natal planets with respect to the transiting outer planets or slower moving planets such as Saturn and Jupiter are also very important and prominent in the astrological community.

Astronomically, cycles are related to the speed of the planetary movements. The impact of a planetary cycle varies as the faster-moving planet crosses various phases forming different geometrical and astronomical relationships with the slower-moving planet. The most fascinating facet is the different flavors of archetypal meaning that we get to experience during the planetary cycles, which involve the current position of one planet and the natal position of another planet.

As Richard Tarnas explains in *Cosmos and Psyche*, "If both the timing of a particular life event and its archetypal quality are found to correlate with the appropriate planetary transits across the appropriate natal planetary positions, the possible implications can more readily be assessed."[1]

All planetary phases are based on the Moon's relationship with the Sun, called the soli-lunar cycle, which starts with the new moon phase and completes with the balsamic phase. Regardless of the two planets or cosmic bodies you observe in a cycle, the basic cycle and phase development are the same. There is always a new beginning, a waxing or growing period, a fullness or culmination, a waning or decreasing period, and an ending or closing. We experience this in all areas of life, including in our gardens, projects, relationships, and our own life and death.

DETERMINING PLANETARY PHASES

To determine which phase two planets are in, start with the slower-moving planet and count by degree counterclockwise until you reach the second planet. The list of planets from fastest to slowest is: Moon, Mercury, Venus, Mars, Jupiter, Saturn, Uranus, Neptune, and Pluto. There are differing opinions about where the Sun belongs in this order. In its relationship with the Moon, the Sun is the slower-moving planet or body. The degrees between the two reveal the phase.

For example, let's calculate a natal Moon-Mercury phase. First, we locate Mercury (the slower of the two) in the birth chart. To make it simple, let's say Mercury is 1 degree Gemini. Now find the Moon (the faster-moving planet). Let's say the Moon is 1 degree Libra. Since there are 30 degrees in each sign, Gemini (the third sign) to Libra (the seventh sign) passes four signs, 30 degrees each. So 1 degree Gemini to 1 degree Libra equals 120 degrees apart. As you can see in Moon Phases and Their Energies, 120 degrees is in the waxing half of the cycle in the first quarter phase.

There are eight phases, each of them encompassing 45 degrees of the 360-degree zodiac. The first four phases are the waxing phases or waxing hemicycle. The waxing hemicycle is associated with *subjective awareness*, which means looking at life from a personal perspective. The view is through a personal lens with a tendency to see the world in terms of how it makes us feel or what it does *to* us. The final four phases are the waning phases or waning hemicycle. The waning hemicycle is associated with *objective awareness*, which is a broader perspective that considers what others and life are doing on their own accord.

In chapters 2 to 10, we explain these phases in much more depth. And while the planetary functions and integration vary in each chapter, the eight phases do not. The phases faithfully repeat, and if you keep reading until the end, you'll be fully immersed in them!

MOON PHASES AND THEIR ENERGIES

Phase	*Energies*
1. New Phase / Waxing / 0–45 degrees	Emergence Starting a new cycle or frame of experience Instinctual, spontaneous, impulsive Charging forward with no to little external light for guidance Driven to experience and initiate Freedom to try it out
2. Crescent Phase / Waxing / 45–90 degrees	Expansion Struggle to give and recognize value, meaning, and purpose The old challenges the new Intense struggle to get out of old patterns Determination, exhaustion, focus Embodiment of what was initiated in prior phase

Phase	*Energies*
3. First Quarter / Waxing / 90–135 degrees	Action Forceful activity without much forethought Testing things out to see what works Results of action hit you right in the face Subjective and may not own results Taking the show on the road
4. Gibbous / Waxing / 135–180 degrees	Overcoming Self-analysis leading to self-improvement Potential for shifts in perception Tight mental activity and struggle to release criticism Developing techniques and tools Stepping back to adjust, improve, perfect, and fine-tune
5. Full / Waning / 180–225 degrees	Fulfillment, completion, fruition Culmination or the inability to go on Learning through the mirror and may project onto others Social and intellectual emphasis, focus on relationship The results of the entire waxing cycle are visible Recognizing and learning what to do with the results
6. Disseminating / Waning / 225–270 degrees	Demonstration—presenting and making use of what you've learned Working within the rules and structure of society Sharing knowledge and wisdom Making results useful and meaningful to society Conditioned responses break down Reaching maximum growth point and recognizing it

Phase	*Energies*
7. Last Quarter / Waning / 270–315 degrees	Reorientation Self in context of the greater good Pinnacle of self-identity and individuation Accepting responsibility for actions and understanding results Insight, innovation, liberation from the past Last push to reach a successful outcome
8. Balsamic / Waning / 315–360 degrees	Release Closing phase—reaching the end or dying Sense of social destiny and urge to sacrifice Slowing down, withdrawing, receding, fading, dissolving Letting go of the past and surrendering to the unknown Preparing to produce the seed that will birth the new cycle

APPLYING PLANETARY PHASES IN PRACTICE

Any significant configuration in the birth chart indicates a particular manifestation or a condition in both tangible and intangible ways. Tangible is an actual manifestation that takes place in the form of a life event. Intangible is a feeling that arises due to a specific configuration that's prominent in the individual. So how do these configurations in the birth chart manifest and when do they manifest? A modern astrologer would look at the transits and progressions while a traditional astrologer would look at the time-lord systems along with a few other traditional predictive techniques. In any way, the configuration in the birth chart needs to be activated in some manner.

Robert Hand once said the most prominent transit is first felt at the heart on an inner level.[2] For example, a Mars-Saturn opposition would likely drain all the energy inside us and put us through some uncomfortable situations. We're not determining this to be positive or negative, just as something happening. When it comes to transits and working with phases, identify a planet as constant and the Moon as variable.

Let's look at Mars as an example. If Mars is in Capricorn, the cycle begins when the Moon conjuncts Mars in Capricorn. The Moon will quickly move from one sign to another and the progress of the Moon across the signs will take it through the different phases (new, crescent, first quarter, gibbous, full, disseminating, last quarter, and balsamic). Each phase in the transit will have a particular psychological effect on the individual at the inner level, to a minimal extent if not a great impact. For deeper information, we'd need to study other various factors.

The phases express similarly in the natal and secondary progressed charts, the time periods just vary. An individual with a natal Moon-Jupiter new phase conjunction will continue to exhibit the qualities and nature of this conjunction throughout their life. However, for those who don't have the conjunction in their birth chart, when their progressed Moon meets natal Jupiter, it begins a new phase that will include all the qualities of the Moon-Jupiter natal conjunction. These qualities may not be found in these individuals by birth, but they pick up and activate as they move through the phases by progression. Using this technique in progressions adds critical insight into the individuals' development as it's evolving.

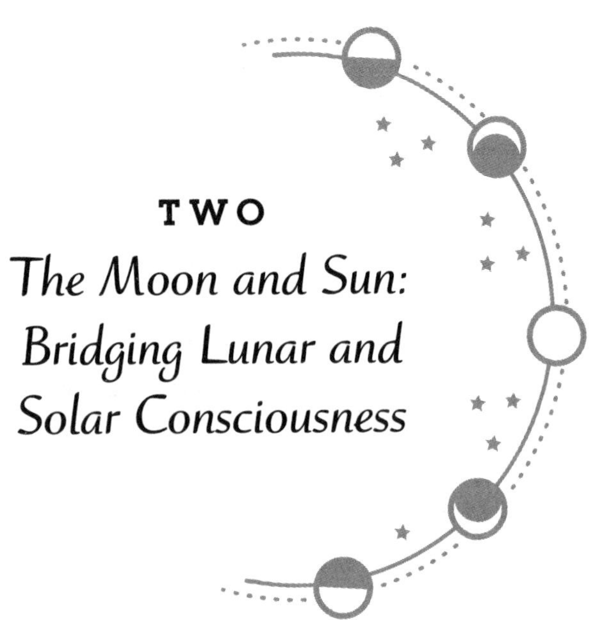

TWO
The Moon and Sun: Bridging Lunar and Solar Consciousness

We often ask or wonder, "Who am I?" or "What is my purpose?" Our lower minds love answers, all wrapped up with a pretty bow. And although we can answer these questions to some extent and have tools such as astrology to help us dig deeper and gain more understanding, nothing replaces experience … ever. Only by living do we discover more of who we are and the path of dharma unique to us. Answers are not meant to be given to us in a reading, counseling session, or through some typology. This is not to discourage anyone from consulting them—they can be revealing, supportive, healing, and empowering. The problem is in solely relying on an external source to define what we are or what we should do.

The Sun and Moon represent our light and the personal way we shine. We don't just mean *shine* as in a simplified showing-off of oneself. Our personal energy emits a frequency that interacts with all creation unlike anything or anyone else. That energy, or light, radiates within us and without. It can brighten the darkness, warm the cold, and heal simply with its emanation. There are people, animals, plants, and beings of all kinds that benefit from your energetic beingness. Even when you aren't doing anything, your presence on this planet and in the universe contributes to the well-being of everything.

When you live your Sun and Moon as fully as you can, beaming your most genuine self, every cell in your body aligns with the vibration. You may never have the words to describe this energy of yours, but you feel it; you just are it. The more you allow yourself to unfold naturally, following your heart and committing to the integrity of your authenticity, the stronger your frequency becomes. As humans, we'll never completely embody our energy—to do so would transform us into pure light. We're here to glow through this flesh and skin, but we can hold and radiate much more of ourselves than most of us do. There's no greater contribution or calling than to be and do you, and that's an unfolding process; sometimes hidden, sometimes revealing, always changing… much like our Sun and Moon.

THE RELATIONSHIP BETWEEN THE MOON AND SUN

The lunation cycle is the dance between the Sun and Moon, known as the soli-lunar phases. The mystery of the Moon's phases and changing faces is romanticized all around the world. We look up at the sky and exclaim what a beautiful bright Moon, but the Moon isn't doing any of that by itself. Rarely do we stop and acknowledge the Sun's role in lighting the night sky, but we do so here because astrology is all about relationships. What we see in the waning, waxing, or full moon is the relationship between the Sun and Moon. The Sun, the star in our solar system, generates light and the Moon reflects it. This is a magical, beautiful relationship, astronomically and metaphysically.

We can't look directly at the Sun without damaging our eyesight, but we can gaze upon its light in the mirror of the Moon. Moonlight *is* sunlight—our luminaries are a very literal representation of yin and yang or polarity. Metaphorically, every month at the Sun-Moon conjunction or new moon, the Sun infuses the Moon with its vital energy and the Moon absorbs it and sends it down to us on Earth. The Moon makes the Sun's life force digestible so we can receive it in our human form—the Sun is so powerful it would blow our circuits without a filter. The nature of this energy changes monthly as the Sun and Moon enter different zodiac signs. Every year, we receive the full spectrum of solar energy, from Aries through Pisces, through the body of the Moon. This itself is reason enough to call her Mother, but gender doesn't matter. The point is, the Moon is our energetic life vessel. This concept is also true within you, in the relationship between your personal Sun, Moon, and soli-lunar phase.

In his profound book, *The Lunation Cycle*, Dane Rudhyar emphasizes that your lunation birthday, the soli-lunar phase you were born under, is just as important as your Sun, Moon, or Rising signs.[3] He explains the Sun as our basic archetypal purpose and the soli-lunar phase as how we're working this out and living it. So the Sun and Moon together are how we actualize our sense of purpose in our physical lives. Most of us don't go running around saying, "I'm a New Moon Phase," but maybe we should. It's a key to how we're meant to do our special thing on this planet.

LIGHT-GENERATING SUN

The Sun is a star and that's already making a bold statement. It doesn't orbit around anything, and stars are held together by their own gravity. There are many schools of astrology and many ways to practice, but most of us agree that the Sun is a symbol of the central purpose in a person's life, just as it's the center of our solar system. The sign your natal Sun is in shows the energy you need to keep generating and beaming to stay healthy, motivated, and happy. The Sun corresponds with our intellectual nature, the part of us that works with rationale, reason, and linearity. It wants us to be something and get somewhere and holds those ideals close to the heart. The Sun also represents integration, weaving everything else in the chart together. The Sun in you wants to make you proud and has something special to contribute to the world.

Stars are essentially exploding balls of gas that produce energy, making them HOT. Our Sun is about 10,000 degrees Fahrenheit, but other stars are far hotter. And scientists have proven that we humans are made of stardust, so no surprise the Sun sign is the star of astrology. The Sun is vital energy, like the type of fuel you run on. You won't go anywhere when the tank's empty, and filling it up with the wrong fuel for your engine won't work either. If we don't live by the calling of our Sun, our light goes out, and eventually, we burn out. The Sun represents our hero's journey; our personal myth. If your hero is Sagittarius, you'll need different experiences and challenges than a Cancer, but the quest is basically the same. We're all on a journey of self-discovery and the Sun is the leading role. Who and what we are is enlivened by the Sun. Our Sun is our prana, life force, spirit. In Stoic philosophy, cultivating the divine spark within and fulfilling our own nature is the purpose of our lives. Just as the Sun shines in the sky, doing exactly what it was created to do, we just need to be who we are, pure and simple. We are all suns becoming, individually and collectively.

CYCLES OF THE MOON AND SUN

The Sun represents our solar consciousness or daytime selves. When we set goals and work to fulfill our potential, we're in the Sun's domain. The Moon represents our lunar consciousness or nighttime selves. The inner world of feelings, dreams, and mystery is the Moon's realm. Together, the two merge the inside and out; heart and intellect. A whole human is both day and night; light and dark. Throughout this book, we talk about the Moon as heart and how nothing can stop you when your heart truly desires something. That's the deal with the Sun and Moon. Even if your Sun-self can visualize the grand purpose of your existence and how to achieve it step by step, if your heart's not in it, that purpose will live as an idea and never materialize in the earth realm. We need the Moon as creator and guardian of flesh and blood to keep the spirit in the body and nurture its growth from sunrise to sunset; birth to death.

Working with your natal soli-lunar phase is a powerful way to reconnect with the growth approach that works best for you. Whenever you know what you want or need to do, whatever it is, the energy of your soli-lunar phase is how you can best do it. If you were born under a first quarter moon, you need to test things out and learn how they work by doing them. You need to go for it. You can also work with soli-lunar phases in secondary progressions. The phase of your progressed Moon and Sun can help you understand where you are in the current cycle of actualizing your potential. As with everything in astrology and life, consciously working *with* energy expands potential and transforms obstacles into opportunities.

BRIDGING LUNAR AND SOLAR CONSCIOUSNESS

With the luminaries, we're exploring a relationship that's different from the Moon with the other planets. The Sun and Moon are not technically planets and therefore are not free agents like Mercury, Venus, Mars, Jupiter, Saturn, Uranus, Neptune, and Pluto. The Sun and Moon are a team, even more than that, a sacred union or marriage of energy. They're the lights, the light within and the light without. The Sun gives light—asserting. The Moon takes and reflects light—receiving. The integration of giving and receiving light and energy is what creates life. Sun and Moon together show how you're naturally wired to create and receive yourself and everything around you.

If you have a Taurus Sun, you generate stable, abundant, enduring energy. You're creating yourself through the mysteries of Taurus. Your output is Taurus. If you have a Cancer Moon, all that beautiful, grounded, growing power of Taurus is received by gentle, nurturing, and healing Cancer. The Moon is naturally a supportive function, and when you play the Moon to your own Sun, it's a win for both the day and night within you. And, finally, if your soli-lunar phase is crescent, you're working out this whole thing called life by struggling through the tension between the old and new. You're building a foundation for what's to come. Expansion is your theme and it's not easy. You must embody what you've initiated.

Sometimes the ways we use our energy in the external world zaps our internal resources. Other times, the obsession with our inner world doesn't leave any energy to be shared with anyone or anything around us. We all have the sense that we're destined for something great (even if we've suppressed or repressed it) and have the desire to follow that prompting. At the same time, we all need to feel safe at home, with people who love us. We all long to pursue our personal paths and be part of the family. This duality of leaving and returning is the interplay of the soul's evolution. The Sun and Moon constantly, at their greatest expression, are the in-breath of our fullest potential and the exhale of release to what is and has always been. We are both, and the Sun and Moon show us the way we've chosen to experience it in this lifetime. They let us consciously perceive the spirit in matter that we are and leave our mark in this mortal coil.

MOON-SUN PHASES

NEW PHASE (0–45 DEGREES APART) AND THE NEW CONJUNCTION

Individuals born during the soli-lunar new phase are starting, or have recently started, a new evolutionary cycle when it comes to living their purpose. We can also look at this as the birth of a new way of living. An entirely new frame of experience is unfolding and there is no way to begin something other than taking the first leap. In the sky, this is new moon, just as or after the Moon and Sun come together, kicking off the monthly lunar cycle. The Moon appears dark or as only a thin sliver in our sky, but it's just been infused with the Sun's light and will release that energy throughout the following phases until it meets the Sun again. These individuals need to approach life with spontaneity. They're learning to trust their instincts and see where it leads. With very little external light to guide them, their inner knowing is their compass and when they recognize and follow it, synchronicity and serendipity abound. Just like a two-year-old isn't interested in other people's opinions, new phase people do better in the "driver's seat" as a general life approach. They need authenticity and autonomy.

We traditionally set intentions under the new moon because it represents infinite potential and the creative spark that ignites our desires. With its Arien quality, new phase carries a warrior vibration; the fight to exist and stay alive—to initiate a new chapter in the book of life and keep it going, so it can develop into its fullest expression. It does take the force of the Aries ram to charge into the next phase, like watching springtime plants sprout through the frozen earth to reach the light of day. Emergence requires a tremendous amount of energy, and individuals in this phase often have a fiery vitality. They can be antsy, impulsive, and reactive. That's their nature. The drive to experience life and oneself is strong—a new life beckons and to ignore the call brings depression, anger, and boredom. Even when it's terrifying, the only way forward is by doing. Fears of not knowing where to go or what will happen are common, but reassurance is found by affirming that the new phase is new. Individuals in this phase aren't supposed to have it all figured out. They need the freedom to try, blurt it out, and fly forward without worrying about how it will look or end up. All we know for sure at this point is that failure to launch is the real danger because the entire future depends on getting in the game now.

CRESCENT PHASE (45–90 DEGREES APART)

The Moon has moved far enough away from the Sun in the crescent phase to be a substantial crescent of light in the sky, even coming close to a half-moon toward the later degrees. What was initiated in the new phase is ready for expansion, which requires stability, grounding, and determination. Individuals with this natal phase are working hard to make something of themselves. This is past the adventurous beginning, but not yet anchored firmly. If this were a wild horse, it would be caught in the corral, but not broken for riding. If it could, it would escape and go back to the wild. People in this phase are facing the patterns and ways of the past and struggling to keep their new, forward motion going. With its Taurean flavor, the soli-lunar crescent phase is the challenge to recognize the value in a new way of living. These individuals live their purpose by taking steady steps toward their goals and proving their worth. Their focus and endurance are almost unyielding when they can see the results of their efforts.

Establishing anything can be exhausting and the soli-lunar crescent phase is an initiation into building like no other. Even if this isn't a material realm project, it's the energetic and emotional equivalent of manual labor. It's easy to get stuck, especially when each step takes so long, and everything starts to feel futile. This is when individuals in this phase need to appreciate their progress more than ever. It's easy to look at a house and admire its beautiful architecture without giving a thought to the foundation. Nothing would stand without the foundation. Similarly, a tree is dependent on the anchoring of its roots or it collapses. We're quick to dismiss what we don't see, but the unseen is almost always the vital part. Crescent phase people need to cultivate deep, unwavering self-love and put their full weight down on themselves. They can and need to hold and build themselves up. This is a phase of embodiment. The free spirit raw energy of the previous new phase needs containment and definition so it can become something usable and sustainable. The soli-lunar crescent phase is the honor of holding, supporting, and securing what has meaning. Individuals born in this phase need to invest their time, resources, and heart into what is truly worthy.

FIRST QUARTER PHASE (90–135 DEGREES APART)

The soli-lunar first quarter phase is dynamic and generative, very much like Leo, its associated sign. The waxing moon is at least half full and quite noticeable in the sky. This phase begins with the first quarter square, and squares are always a challenge. When working with the Moon and Sun, the challenge is very personal; between private emotional needs and a sense of identity and purpose in the world. It's an opportunity for the private and public selves to integrate in a new way. Individuals in this phase are impelled to take action and show off their stuff. They need to give it their best shot and get immediate feedback. This isn't a thoughtful or practical approach on its own—other signatures in the chart always must be considered. This is an "act in the moment of passion" phase. Anything less than wholehearted just feels empty. Of course, there will be times when it doesn't work out so well, and the best approach is to be objective and correct course ... something individuals in this phase are learning.

Anything associated with Leo tends to get a bad rap and it's worth exploring this for a minute. If we stop to consider the motivation of this sign and what it must go through to evolve, we're less likely to judge outward behavior, even when it's unbearably self-centric. Leo and first quarter phase signatures need to be seen, and it's not enough just to show up, it must be vulnerable. If you've ever had to speak at a meaningful event, such as a wedding reception or memorial service, or performed a talent in front of an audience, you know what we mean. It's scary, and most of us do care what it looks like and if other people like it. Soli-lunar first quarter phase people live their life purpose by sharing their talents, creations, and what's in their hearts. The pitfall can be refusing to own their actions and blaming others or becoming overly attached to approval and applause. The beauty in this phase is the vibrant, creative energy that can't help but express excitement. Individuals in this phase won't be the star of every show, but they entertain us and inspire us to share our own creativity. The childlike exuberance is contagious and helps us all shine.

GIBBOUS PHASE (135–180 DEGREES APART)

The soli-lunar gibbous phase is the final waxing phase. When we consider the phases as development over time, this one is critical because it's like a dress rehearsal. Anyone born in this phase has an agenda, conscious or not, to get themselves together and get it right. In the sky, the Moon is almost full and there's an impending sense of wonder that something magical is about to be revealed. But, not yet. This is the last call to change the shape or construction of the thing that's been growing since the new phase. Gibbous is a phase of crisis through self-analysis—questioning one's purpose and the ability to live it and do it well enough. Individuals in this natal phase are not easy on themselves, finding it hard to forgive themselves for previous actions or inaction. They can best live their purpose by improving what they can and putting their energy into what's useful and really makes a difference.

Gibbous phase people will often blame themselves for any shortcomings and assume guilt that's not theirs to bear. Yes, it's important to do our best and make things better when possible, but sometimes, there's only so much we can do. Doing our best is all we can do, and it is enough. As these individuals come to understand themselves better, they, in turn, have a greater understanding of humanity and the feelings of inadequacy we all experience. With its Virgoan quality, gibbous phase brings the potential for improvement on all levels: mind, body, and spirit. Healing is a path some soli-lunar gibbous phase people take, and they can be highly successful at creating and implementing various tools and techniques for a wide range of purposes. Perfection can become an obsession, along with continually finding problems, which is obviously problematic. But in healthy doses, this is the motivation to refine and prepare oneself, and whatever's been growing, for the following full phase; the culmination of all efforts since the initiation at the new phase.

FULL PHASE (180–225 DEGREES APART) AND THE OPPOSITION

In the soli-lunar full phase, the Moon is the biggest and brightest, symbolizing illumination, awareness, and fulfillment. Full phase begins when the Moon is 180 degrees from the Sun, reflecting the maximum light. The Moon has reached its limits of fullness and now the waning cycle begins. Full phase individuals have reached a state of culmination in developing something in the journey of living their life purpose. They've just released something, or a version of themselves, into the world and now it's out there. It's time to see it from a clear and broad perspective and put it to meaningful use. There's always the potential that the result of efforts (that is, everything developed or grown through the first half of the cycle) can't or won't reach its potential for meaningfulness. Intentions don't always work out, and in these cases, the remaining waning cycle is spent learning, accepting, and letting go. Either way, the word "full" implies capacity, and individuals can't keep going on in the same evolutionary container. It's like graduating from a program. When you graduate, those months or years of education are over. What you do with it and make of it is up to you.

Full moons are legendary across cultures and time. We associate them with romance, magic, and madness. The word *lunacy* and *lunatic* can be translated as "insanity," but that definition is subjective. When the Moon is full, it brings things into the light, often what's been hidden or partially obscured. This can be like suddenly seeing or realizing something about yourself or someone else for the first time. Awareness can be beautiful and enlightening or upsetting and confusing, depending on how we respond to it. Full phase is the halfway point in the lunar cycle, a shift from subjective to objective awareness. This is a new beginning in consciousness; being able to see others and life as it is, without always personalizing. Objective is not better or more evolved than subjective. They're different perspectives or orientations. If we don't fully develop ourselves personally, we won't have a whole self to contribute to relationships and society. Full phase is the initiation into equal partnerships, true cooperation, and union.

Those born during this phase have a natural attunement with Libran qualities, the sign that corresponds with full phase and the opposition aspect. Just as the Moon mirrors the Sun's light in the sky, these individuals are learning about who they are through others. They need to engage life socially and intellectually. Who they attract and what they find around them reflects who they are, especially their own unintegrated parts or shadow side. It's easy to project limitations and expectations onto others in this phase, and to see and operate in extremes.

All planetary aspects are about integration, but the opposition is the most obvious example because it involves polarities. Polarities aren't two different things, they're one continuum of energy. For example, Aries/Libra is the continuum of relationship experienced from opposite points of view. Aries and Libra are incomplete without each other; they don't even exist without each other. Polarities and the opposition embody inherent tension, and tension is the only way to come into balance. Imagine a tightrope with slack on both ends or two people on a seesaw sitting on the same side. Balance is more than one thing coming together, each holding its own while adjusting to get the proportions right—a Libran skill. Individuals in this phase need to work with others to reach a sense of completion, inside and out. Interconnectedness is a theme that weaves through everything. They can best live their life purpose by growing through relationships and exploring the natural Hermetic Law of Correspondence: "As above, so below," which can also be understood as "as within, so without."[4]

DISSEMINATING PHASE (225–270 DEGREES APART)

In the soli-lunar disseminating phase, the Moon is waning, but still a strong presence in the sky. Individuals born under this phase are seeking to contribute to society in a meaningful way. They need to achieve something with whatever talents and skills they were born with or developed. The Capricornian energy of this phase has a serious and practical edge that isn't satisfied with anything less than solid, productive, respectable results. Whatever reached maturity with the full phase must be applied in a useful way.

The aim here is to demonstrate what's been learned through the previous phases and share that wisdom with society. Capricorn embodies accountability, integrity, practicality, and the ability to see the bigger picture and orchestrate everything into efficiency. Disseminating phase people are often concerned with building a legacy and willing to work to the bone tirelessly in the process. They have the responsibility of taking what they've created, with all the resources available to them, and pushing it to the pinnacle of functionality. These individuals need to use their gifts of leadership and manifestation to help themselves and others reach the heights of potential.

Making things useful to society means working within society's structures and rules. Individuals in the disseminating phase are faced with conditioning, and while they must operate in the "machine," they're also recognizing the limits and restrictions that inherently come with the territory. A true wise one meets people where they're at and inspires them to consider a different future. At their best, disseminating phase people are agents for change that can slowly turn the ship in a new direction. They aren't hasty, so the baby isn't thrown out with the bathwater. The past is not something to discard; it's something to learn from, build on, and improve upon. Sometimes, we're impatient, wanting immediate results and a pill to cure everything. When we don't like something, we want to rip it out of existence and start over. But there's a better way, and the disseminating phase is an invitation to play by the rules long enough to fully understand them and how they came to be. This is the only way to accomplish the great work of moving our planet to a new level of existence. People listen to those who've been in the trenches and reached their position through hard work and life experience. There's a danger of getting lost in the game but it's worth the risk. Only by playing can you win and only from going inside can you bring anyone out, or up. This phase is the ultimate summit and these individuals are called to rise and respond.

LAST QUARTER PHASE (270–315 DEGREES APART)

The soli-lunar last quarter phase is the challenge of re-orientation. Just like the last quarter square that begins this phase, this is a crisis in consciousness. The entire soli-lunar cycle is reaching the end and now the individual must accept responsibility for actions and realize the deeper meaning of his or her choices. Aquarian energy permeates this phase and we can't work with Aquarius without confronting our authenticity, or lack thereof. People born in this phase are naturally rebellious in one way or another, often rebelling against their own patterns and rules. It takes time and perspective to see what we truly are, and by the last quarter phase, the Moon has moved far enough away from the Sun to be more of a free agent in observation. In the sky, the Moon is half full, but it's waning, so more accurately half empty. There's enough light to work with, but it's on its way out. Time is critical and individuals in this phase feel the shift to liberate from the past and give the future the best chance. They need to understand who they are, and it can be shocking to discover the truth, almost like an identity crisis. Beyond that, they need to experience themselves as a member of the world, in the context of the greater good.

Anything conservative retained from the previous phases is now under review. The outcome we've been working with in the past two phases is pretty much fixed, but now, the individual's insight and ideas about the whole process gain merit all on their own. Even if the current cycle won't be improved, the response to and awareness of it begin to infuse the mind and spirit with hope and inspiration for what's coming next. To get the most value out of this phase, beliefs must be embodied—it's not enough to talk about it or grasp it intellectually. When a person in this phase realizes what they honestly value and stand for, they're impelled to prove it by being that person in word and deed. There's a radical streak in people born in this phase and they can act as the last drop in the bucket. They have the power to push stagnant, confining situations over the top, so there's room for new content to fill the space. There are some things we can't change, but why focus on that when there's so much we can? The final phase is approaching, and this is the last chance to reach a successful outcome. A successful outcome here is defined by breakthroughs that strike like lightning, awakening consciousness. This electrifying clears away anything old that can't withstand, short circuits it in its tracks, and establishes a new current. The person who reaches this point becomes this new current and can gift that frequency. Last quarter phase people need to approach life with creative solutions, a genuine desire to heal the planet and help humanity, and a willingness to reinvent themselves.

BALSAMIC PHASE (315–360 DEGREES APART) AND THE BALSAMIC CONJUNCTION

The soli-lunar balsamic phase is the ending of the entire cycle. The Moon is about to complete its orbit around Earth and return to meet the Sun (as close as they come). With less distance between the Moon and Sun, the Moon becomes a thin sliver and then dark. We often call the balsamic moon the dying moon and those born during this phase feel it; time is running out and something is almost over. With its Piscean quality, the balsamic phase is mystical and spiritual. We don't know what happens or comes after we die, and this phase draws us toward that mystery. These individuals need to spend time withdrawn from the external world to listen to their inner voice and connect with something greater than themselves. The more attached the person is to the material world and finite existence, the more dreadful and hopeless this phase can seem. When we don't believe there will be a new beginning after an ending, it's easy to give up or try and keep it going forever. Either way, it's a fight against the inevitable. Balsamic phase people need to let go and surrender into the future. It takes faith and courage to release the past and step into the unknown. In the end, there's no other way. We all enter the void.

Something very powerful happens when we know we're coming to an end. It's like learning you have a terminal disease and have two months to live. Some people throw in the towel, become bitter, and just want it to be over. Others come truly alive for the first time and do everything they can to embrace and celebrate each moment. Sometimes we need to face death to appreciate life. Balsamic phase people can live as though they were dying, for better or worse. This phase brings a sense of social destiny that can motivate great acts of compassion and the urge to sacrifice for humanity. Because there's a natural disintegration or fading away of one's world, disillusionment and disappointment are common. What was once so real and true now vaporizes. It's as if these individuals have each foot in different worlds, which can inspire creativity and vision or threaten their sanity.

Soli-lunar balsamic phase people live their purpose by letting go of the past and preparing for the future. They need to forgive themselves and others and bring things to closure. As they burn through old karma, they create spaciousness within and without. Imagine a huge heap of rubbish belonging to a homeless person—homelessness is a state of transition or space between. Everything they own is in that pile and to the average person, it's hard to see the value amidst the dirt and deterioration. We're all like that—although our junk isn't always on display. Just like the dump or a compost pile, the balsamic phase holds the leftovers of the entire cycle. Individuals in this phase need to clear out anything that will not serve the future. This includes thoughts, beliefs, habits, attachments, and writing off old debts so they won't be recycled. Beginnings are always dependent on the previous ending. The old provides the seed for the new. How we end something energetically imprints what's to come next. Even when they're young, balsamic phase people can feel old, and cyclically speaking, they are senior citizens. They're deciding how they want to be remembered, what really matters, what to leave behind, and how they can give of themselves to help grow generations to come. They know somewhere deep down that whatever isn't resolved in this life will be met in another.

THREE
The Moon and Mercury: Bridging Heart and Mind

As we look closely at the cycle of the Moon and Mercury from a psychological point of view, we've come to realize this is an evolution of the human mind—that is, the mind dealing with the call of both logical and emotional intelligences. This cycle is a study of psychological growth as a person keeps on learning in life. We're all influenced by various factors in this living existence, which can in part be observed and understood with the Moon's progress or motion away from Mercury. But learning is a never-ending process and the wisdom and experience a person attains as and when the Moon's progress happens is the road to excellence. The heart is always leading us to yet another cycle of the Moon and Mercury.

There are many ideas about the mind and its relationship with the Moon and Mercury. The Moon is understood as mind in Vedic astrology. In Western astrology, we're quick to bring Mercury forward anytime the word *mind* comes up, but what do we mean by *mind*? The general definition is the part of us that thinks and feels; the part that allows us to be aware, which is often called consciousness. Gregg Henriques, PhD, author of *A New Unified Theory of Psychology,* defines the mind as the flow of information through the nervous system.[5] He explains that the flow of information can be separated from the biophysical matter that makes up the nervous system. Dr. Henriques offers the analogy of a book. A book's mass and physical dimensions are the brain. The information the book contains is the mind. He further adds that consciousness is "experienced" information flow, but we don't know how to create that experience. We can't engineer consciousness.

If the mind is the flow of information through the nervous system, it makes sense that both the Moon and Mercury are a major part of it from an astrological perspective. Traditionally, we know the Moon corresponds with the subconscious mind and sympathetic nervous system (fight-flight-freeze response). Mercury is also associated with the nervous system and all the transmissions and connections of messages and signals throughout the body. Both the Moon and Mercury are reactive and responsive to stimuli in the internal and external environment. The Moon and Mercury reflect our thinking and feeling in response to life as it happens. But we can't find thoughts or feelings ... seriously, no one has been able to tangibly isolate one. We can't cut ourselves open and find them or pull them in from the energy field to examine them. The mind is kind of an illusion. It can't be found.

If we look at the mind as the culmination of perceiving, it gets even less factual. Perception is personal, subjective, and quick to change. One hundred people can experience the same thing and their perspective will vary greatly. In astrology, the Moon and

Mercury teach us about these personalized experiences—how we respond, feel, and make sense of things. Our perception of and reaction to life frames our reality. How we feel and think about things is powerful. The Buddha teaches that all we are is a result of our thoughts. These thoughts come from both the mind of the head (Mercury) and the mind of the heart (Moon). But the Moon and Mercury play the mind game differently, and sometimes it seems like they're on different teams.

THE EMOTIONAL MOON MIND

The Moon, or emotional mind, is pushed by the heart. It wants care, trust, and security. It's always looking for comfort and belonging. The Moon is the process of emotion, and evolutionary astrology teaches that evolution only happens through the emotional body. But the emotional process involves the mental body because emotions are the result of body (sensation), mind (thinking), and heart (feeling) coming together. This just adds to the mysterious nature of the Moon; the mysterious nature of ourselves. Ancient Hindu teachings tell us that the real knower (soul) of all mind and matter is hidden in the heart. And the Moon, our heart and spirit, houses the soul's emotional experience of the past. It's also integrating the past and future in the present. It's the most personal part of the chart.

When you're talking with someone, it's always their Moon that's instinctually processing and responding to everything you do, say, and energetically emanate. Being a "moon whisperer" is such an important quality for anyone practicing in the counseling profession. The Moon is our flow, and the movement of that river is impossible to stop. The heart wants what it wants. In some mystical way, the soul or Self lives in the inner chamber of the heart. And it is not bound by the physical body.

THE RATIONAL MERCURY MIND

Mercury, or the rational mind, is perhaps the greatest protector of the ego or self-image. Making sense of things, having the answers, and being able to define everything we encounter keeps us feeling safe. An addiction to knowing is something most of us can relate to. The unknown brings up fear, so it's easy to stay the same and avoid the risk. This is a very limited view of Mercury, but it's important to address it because our thoughts do create reality. What we think and say, along with our emotions, are running the show. Stop for a minute and be honest about what runs through your head most of each day. That's what is getting your attention.

Mercury is an amazing tool at our disposal. In the tarot, Mercury is The Magician card, wielding his wand with perfect timing. He's mastered his own creative thinking mind, and in the process learned to influence the minds of others. We can look at Mercury as not just the logical mind, but also the presence of mind or the intellectual ability to be aware that we are thinking and feeling. It's our identification with the mind. It's well summarized in the quote by René Descartes: "Cogito, ergo sum," which translates to "I think, therefore I am."[6] Mercury in the birth chart and in transits and progressions reveals the story we're creating moment to moment based on what we *believe* is happening. It's our perspective and the way we connect the dots. It's easy to over-identify with what we think, to the point that we give our minds control. Just as in mythology, Mercury is the messenger. But he is not the message. He can get just about anything to go anywhere he wants (just like our thoughts), but it's a tricky business. We humans are good at making meaning out of things, and that meaning is often not true.

MOON AND MERCURY INTERACT

The Moon and Mercury are the fastest movers in our solar system, just like the heart and head, and the nervous system. Neither the Moon nor Mercury has much patience, and both are always in transition. They're all over the place, even in relation to each other, and this interplay between feeling and logic can be very inconsistent. The Moon is always moving away from Mercury like the tide. Mercury wants to figure everything out, but the Moon is beyond logical reason. The Moon doesn't care if things make sense. It's perfectly happy being a mystery. While the logical mind processes, the heart-mind responds.

In chemistry, mercury does not react with water under normal conditions. Mercury is the denser of the two and sinks to the bottom without dissolving. If we look at the Moon as freshwater, based on traditional correspondence, it doesn't mix with Mercury. They each hold their own integrity in the presence of each other. It's not a heart-mind melding action we're going for, it's a bridge or connection that brings everything together and permits access into areas otherwise not available.

If one of our greatest human superpowers is the energy we call the mind, and that mind is made up of thinking, emotion, and all perception, how can we consciously work to realize its greatest potential? Playing with the idea that Mercury and the Moon together represent the nervous system and the information flowing through it, how are they working together? We have a brain in the head and a brain in the gut, but which one is running the show, if that is even possible? The nervous system is the body-mind reality, a place most of us live, most of the time. It collects, processes, interprets and responds to all external and internal sensory input. We're so much more than this, but the point of being human is to live in, with, and through this part of us.

CYCLES OF THE MOON AND MERCURY

The Moon and Mercury share a very interesting relationship in many ways. Considering that both are faster-moving planets, exploring the cycles of these planets can be tricky at a basic level because in a planetary cycle, from a transit point of view, a conjunction is formed between a faster- and slower-moving planet in the same sign. The cycle comes to an end when the faster-moving planet comes to the twelfth sign from the position of the slower-moving planet. For example, if Jupiter and the Moon are both in Taurus, the Moon will transit through all the zodiac signs. When it reaches Taurus again, a new cycle begins and the previous cycle ends. The key point here is that the Moon ends its cycle with Jupiter with Jupiter still in Taurus. There is some form of sign-based consistency from Jupiter while the Moon's position and influence is always a variable factor that keeps changing based upon the sign it's in.

However, when it comes to Mercury and the Moon, the Moon moves from one sign to another every 2.25 to 2.5 days and Mercury stays in each sign 14 to 30 days, sometimes even longer depending upon the speed at which it's moving. The Moon completes its cycle in about 29.5 days, whereas Mercury takes 88 days to orbit the Sun, and from a geocentric perspective, takes about a year to go through all twelve signs.

Now, for example, after a Moon-Mercury conjunction in Virgo, the Moon moves across the zodiac signs and by the time it reaches

Leo, Mercury will move into Libra. So the Moon doesn't meet Mercury again in the same sign where their conjunction started (in this example Virgo). Looking at the Moon as an emotional mind and Mercury as a logical mind, we can sense the inconsistency that develops within human beings due to this strange astronomical phenomenon which is less considered.

Consistency in a planetary cycle occurs when the Moon meets the slower-moving planet in the same sign as their previous conjunction (when the slower-moving planet begins and ends the cycle in the same sign). But in the case of the Moon and Mercury, a complete consistent cycle is never reached because Mercury shifts signs before the Moon returns. The energy changes and a new cycle begins with Mercury, the slower-moving planet, in another sign. In the above-mentioned example of the Moon-Mercury conjunction in Virgo, the next new cycle will begin with Mercury in Libra. Nothing stays the same.

This cycle takes an entirely different shift when Mercury goes retrograde. Mercury spends about 45 days in a sign when retrograde and during this time, the Moon completes one full cycle around the zodiac and moves halfway through another. Human emotions and logical reasoning are influenced by a slightly larger cycle with a similar effect, especially when Mercury is in the same sign while appearing to move retrograde.

This relationship between the Moon and Mercury is felt even during transits that activate individual natal charts. While dealing with the progressed Moon and its relationship with Mercury, a significant inconsistency between heart and mind arises when we're forced to make decisions supported by rational or human factors such as emotional attachment, or by both rational and emotional aspects. Understandably, the secondary progression concept (one day equals one year) has more impact because we have more time to work with it, thereby making this an interesting phenomenon to explore.

In the natal chart, the personal Moon-Mercury birth phase is a key to understanding how the mind and the nervous system are coming together in the current cycle of evolutionary development. We can also use the chart to determine whether rational or emotional thinking has been dominant in the past along with the soul's intention for current growth and integration. The personal Moon-Mercury phase can shed light on one's overall relationship with their nervous system—how each of us, as an eternal, boundless spirit is working with human sensations and a body and mind that respond to pleasure and pain. Imagine never having experienced caffeine and drinking a strong cup of coffee. It could be exciting, scary, or make you feel sick. We're all conducting experiments like this every day through our nervous systems. Our circuits are constantly being hit with phenomena. We feel it, label it, judge it, and try to control it.

BRIDGING HEART AND MIND

Exploring the cycles of the Moon and Mercury gives us further insights into how this energy plays in our minds and eventually, in our lives. As we have established our idea of the Moon and Mercury as an emotional mind and logical/presence of mind, respectively, we are applying this differentiation as an underlying factor in the delineation of the cycles of the Moon and Mercury.

Perception and personality are the two most important behavioral aspects that push human life forward in various ways when we look from a psychological point of view. Perception and personality define our attitude toward life. While the Moon moves away from Mercury, we receive the offerings of the sign that the Moon is in. The element, modality or mode, and the nature of the sign have a lot to offer. The Moon's path has a direct bearing on our emotionality. The heart starts feeling various changes as the Moon moves forward in the cycle. Feelings will have a mixed flavor during the cycle. The gap between heart and mind keeps increasing in every phase of the cycle until the opposition. Once the Moon reaches the opposition, there's a clear polarization between the ideas of the logical mind (Mercury) and the heart or emotional mind (Moon). They're just coming at it from different places.

We know that the logical mind and emotional mind are two different aspects of the human mental apparatus. Therefore, it's imperative to understand that our perception and personality keep changing and developing as reflected by the relationship between the Moon and Mercury and the position of the Moon in the various signs. For example, Moon in Aries and Mercury in Sagittarius will create a trine or harmonious relationship between the planets. But in this example, the Moon and Mercury are in the first quarter phase. Keep in mind that this is the first half of the cycle as the Moon is still waxing. Mercury has a slight advantage in terms of dictating logical reasoning over emotional reasoning. In this case, thoughts and feelings do interact with each other, but the emotional mind tends to get lost in the intellect symbolized by Mercury and its position. This is not to emphasize the absence of emotional intelligence. The emotional response is somewhat tied to logic, yet the heart will feel the differences. Here, the sensitivity that the Moon offers and human vulnerability to perception will have an impact on one's personality, which will have an influence in the course of their daily life.

MOON-MERCURY PHASES

NEW PHASE (0–45 DEGREES APART) AND THE NEW CONJUNCTION

The Moon-Mercury new phase is the initiation of an entirely new evolutionary cycle in the relationship between the head and heart. The emotional and logical minds have just come together to initiate a new experience or consciousness that opens the door to a new life. This phase is instinctual and spontaneous. Freedom is needed to try things out and just see what happens. Feeling and thinking are just finding out what it's like to work together in this way. When the emotional mind and logical mind come together in a new phase conjunction, thoughts and feelings are enmeshed. Having just come through the balsamic phase and balsamic conjunction of completion, the two are used to being together, but now the theme is changing, without knowledge of where things are going yet. The ending has transformed into the beginning.

People in this phase tend to be hypersensitive in response to any criticism of their feelings or ideas. In the new phase, it can be difficult to distinguish between emotions (Moon) and thoughts (Mercury). Without much distance between Mercury and the Moon, it's easy for individuals to think they're feeling when they're really intellectualizing and vice-versa. Any perceived attack on their thoughts, reasoning, or feelings is felt and received personally. Objectivity doesn't come naturally. Moon-Mercury new phase people are quite animated in terms of expressing their opinion publicly and very passionate about what they're saying. They tend to converse with their own subconscious as they plan their actions and carry out their life routines.

CRESCENT PHASE (45–90 DEGREES APART)

The Moon-Mercury crescent phase is filled with tension and struggle because the way the head and heart are working together is now past the spontaneous initiation phase and needs to be rooted and recognized as valuable. In this phase, the old and new challenge each other and it takes great determination to keep it going. The call is to expand and focus with each step, even when the going is slow.

This is the first phase where the Moon moves significantly away from Mercury. In other words, even though the heart is largely ruled by the thoughts—which are the result of the combination of emotion and rationale developed by the culmination of heart and mind during the conjunction—an energetic shift has taken place now that the Moon has moved more than 45 degrees away from Mercury. This is where feelings and emotional motivations also have a substantial influence on how the individual is thinking and experiencing daily life.

We're not establishing emotional attachment or logical assumptions as positive or negative by any means here. However, when we begin something, the heart and mind are filled with various rationales to support what we're doing, why we're doing it, how we're doing, and what we'll get in return. In the crescent phase, there can be an emotional attachment to the story we believe and follow. From the other side, there's also a rationale that supports our emotional attachment. Mercury's relationship with the Moon will include more logically backed ideas, even in extremely tricky scenarios. In this phase, individuals can more easily handle emotions because Mercury pushes the Moon with rationalism. This instills courage to manage and bring about some great decision-making. Somewhere between 60 and 90 degrees apart, the distance between the Moon and Mercury increases the potential for conflict resolution and clear communication involving both logic and emotion. This signature can be very helpful to law enforcement and secret agents who are constantly put into extreme situations where they're required to tackle emotions and logic simultaneously.

FIRST QUARTER PHASE (90–135 DEGREES APART)

First quarter is always considered to be a fresh, energetic, and action-oriented phase. The heart and head have been coming together, and now it's time to test it out in the world. Expect to receive the results of actions right in the face—there will be kinks to work out. Individuals will realize that they're clinging to their rational and logical ideologies too much. Challenges between the emotional and logical mind show up in an obvious manner and there's usually an indescribable feeling about the discomfort in sticking to logical principles. However, the individual has little to no conscious realization that they're suppressing their emotional nature and the feelings of the heart. Greater awareness is yet to come.

People in this phase generally excel in random endeavors that don't require upholding the rationale or at times, deadlines. The heart and mind keep jumping from one thing to another and they never really settle in one place. Since there is no limit to imagination and creative ideas, there's potential for tremendous talent in artistic fields. Art and expressing creativity can provide freedom from the limitations of thinking. When Mercury forms a square with the Moon (at the very beginning of the first quarter phase) there can be a sudden, super creative burst. However, there will also be a burden in the mind of perceived logical reality.

Let's explore an example. Say someone wants to become a painter and will need to earn their income from painting. But there's no way a person can start earning a full salary in the initial stages, at least in most cases. Here, the logical mind will force this person to take up another job before feeling confident about generating enough income through painting. Sticking to an old or regular job while starting painting as a side gig is a classic manifestation of the first quarter phase.

GIBBOUS PHASE (135–180 DEGREES APART)

Gibbous is the last phase before the maturity of full phase and is generally focused on addressing inconsistencies between thinking and feeling and everything in between. This is a time of adjustment and change in perspective, with the need to self-analyze to discover a more accurate sense of the mind and its capacity.

Completing and refining the ideas of heart and mind before the opposition aspect is something to work on during this phase. Slowly, a person realizes the emotional side of the mind is getting a hold on them more than usual. This relationship between Mercury and the Moon will bring more shifts in terms of realizing that the logical mind has been suppressing the emotional mind. The nature of this phase helps us reveal that logic is not everything and emotions are valuable. The intellectual mind is not the ruler of the heart.

As writer and lecturer Dale Carnegie stated in his iconic book, *How to Win Friends and Influence People*, "When dealing with people, let us remember we are not dealing with creatures of logic. We are dealing with creatures of emotion."[7]

In the Moon-Mercury gibbous phase, the astronomical relationship between the Moon and Mercury helps individuals make at least one or two decisions against their logical mind and support their emotional mind. They're starting to get the balance right—

giving more value to empathy and feelings. However, this phase is not entirely free from the realm of logic. It's helpful for people in this phase to connect with others to get ideas and opinions about their work and the progress they're making. Gibbous phase is a time to fill in the gaps that the Moon has managed to acquire or avoid on its path thus far.

FULL PHASE (180–225 DEGREES APART) AND THE OPPOSITION

The full phase is the maturity point of the cycle, like a tree bearing fruit. From now on, there's a bit more influence of the heart than the logical mind as this is the initiation of the second half of the entire cycle. This is a classic manifestation of the results of efforts that began during the new phase conjunction. Yet, problems are a byproduct of success. It's either the culmination of achievement to take forward or the impossibility to go on. This is a scenario where the heart and mind can end up having extremely conflicting thoughts. Both the Moon and Mercury will force individual thinking from both dimensions (heart and mind; emotions and logic). Ideas are generated from both sides. There are times when ideas are highly irrational because they're emotional. There are also times when ideas are extremely logical and there is no emotion involved. The opposition is an aspect of extremes coming into balance.

New ideas generated during this period are not always successful and caution should be taken implementing them, because the mind and heart can be far apart from each other. It's very difficult to arrive at a conclusion in terms of choosing heart over mind or mind over heart. People tend to experience the perfect condition of imbalance that brings a challenging task ahead. Therefore, when the transiting Moon opposes natal Mercury, it's better to have someone assist with mediation and collaboration to arrive at a positive outcome with important decisions.

Individuals in the Moon-Mercury full phase can end up making premature decisions at very important junctures in life or never decide at all. They're largely influenced and disturbed by the external environment and the people they come into contact with during daily life. There's a great tendency to project onto others and to see everything as coming from the other side. This is a period to enjoy the success already attained and let time pass before initiating new things. Brainstorming in terms of how to sustain and share accomplishments manifested through the heart-mind relationship is a worthwhile effort.

DISSEMINATING PHASE (225–270 DEGREES APART)

The mind is a gift to the world and in the disseminating phase, it's time to share that wisdom with society. Individual perspective is valuable to others and it's less about the person sharing and more about the people receiving. This is a period of learning to play by society's rules while using personal gifts, so it's important to be careful not to get lost in the game.

In the Moon-Mercury disseminating phase, a maturity develops that allows individuals to share ideas and opinions with others who look up to them. From the other side, this is also a time to come up with more ideas that support the emotional mind, because the inclination is more toward emotion than logic. Psychologist Edward de Bono summed this up when he said, "Most of the mistakes in thinking are inadequacies of perception rather than mistakes of logic."[8] To bring about a balance between both, seeking outside advice is a wise choice. At the same time, the individual must ensure that collective decisions are made instead of giving their authority away exclusively to someone else.

Individuals can recognize how much their opinions are valuable to others, and this phase also brings awareness that the opinions of others help them in the further development of their heart-mind relationship. This is a phase of saturation and mature receptivity. Mercury, our rational mind, makes sure that we're not overly submissive. But being receptive, a quality that comes from the Moon, is equally important. Moon-Mercury disseminating phase people were likely much less receptive during the preceding phases because of the push that Mercury gives to the Moon. But now, the Moon has more voice, which continues to get stronger throughout the remaining second half of the cycle.

LAST QUARTER PHASE (270–315 DEGREES APART)

The last quarter phase calls for reorientation. The mind and the way of reacting and responding to life have become a more integrated part of the person. They're embodying their thoughts and emotions and have the insight to liberate from the past in any way they've become stuck. It's time to accept responsibility for everything that's been done through the union of mind and heart. The entire cycle is almost complete and there's a strong drive to serve the greater good. Moon-Mercury last quarter phase people are naturally more even-minded, wise, and have the capacity for objective awareness. The greater or higher mind can be more accessible with an ability to tune in to a consciousness beyond the ego-mind chatter.

Preceding the balsamic phase, this is the final frontier where there's a chance to put forth the heart before the logical mind, which is a far more grounded "mental" position. Letting go of Mercury's attachment to what the head thinks it knows makes way for the Moon's gifts of empathy and attunement to what the heart truly needs. Individuals in this phase tend to examine their experiences of the past and reanalyze life situations to understand their actions and determine if they can really act on what their heart is communicating. If they're open, they'll hear the heart speaking in awakening and enlightening ways.

BALSAMIC PHASE (315–360 DEGREES APART) AND THE BALSAMIC CONJUNCTION

This is the end of the entire cycle, the final phase where the initial ideas generated from the previous conjunction at the start of the cycle are now coming full circle. The heart is already searching and working toward the next new phase. In the balsamic phase, the voice of the heart can be heard very well. All that's been done with the mind, heart, and head and all the awareness experienced is ready to be passed on. Reality starts fading as the mind, attachment to feelings and thoughts, and the entire way of experiencing life slips away. It's time to let go and prepare for the future by releasing what is no longer useful and offering up anything that will help birth the new cycle to come.

When the planet of emotions, the Moon, forms a balsamic conjunction with the planet of logic, Mercury, there's a culmination of heart and mind. Emotional needs and practical rationale will suddenly come in alignment with the given situation in place. Even without knowing what's going on in the subconscious, the logical mind finds rationale to support wild and spontaneous imaginations that are very much a result of creativity, which is a territory that involves both heart and mind. Individuals in this phase are naturally empathic because empathy is situational even though it is emotional. When a person knows that another fellow human needs empathy, there's a feeling and an underlying rationalization attached to the situation itself that a person needs empathy. There's also an understanding that there's a scope for an opinion or feeling to arise without any conflict between heart and mind or emotions and logic.

Using the painter example from the first quarter phase, the same person in this phase will hear the call of their heart and be motivated to start painting as a main profession. They might finally quit their regular job and pursue their heart's calling. Survival concerns barely enter their mind at this point.

When our heart calls us to do what we love, logic really doesn't come into the picture, especially in the balsamic phase where our heart has a say over the mind. Love wins.

FOUR
The Moon and Venus: Bridging Me and We

Understanding the process of "bridging me and we" through the phases is the path that enables us to understand the intricacies of the most personal and self-oriented consciousness of the human mind, as a separate being and in relationship with others. In the Moon-Venus cycle, we can explore the deeper meanings and motivations of our personal needs and wants from an individual perspective, and also from the perspective of our relationships. We all learn, grow, and evolve through our relationships with various people in life. The Moon's progress, or releasing from Venus, as it moves around the zodiac expands and widens the human experience of feelings and emotions from a relationship standpoint. Understanding the cycle and phases of the Moon and Venus helps us to bring about an optimal balance and healthy compromise between self and others.

The Moon and Venus are both yin archetypes, which automatically create similarities. If we look at the planets as symbols of the parts of the inner psyche, the Moon and Venus are the receptive, responsive, flowing, curving, feeling, and absorbing aspects of our nature. They can both be entirely irrational. If you've "lost your mind" falling in love or spent any time with an immature child, you know what we mean. Traditionally, both the Moon and Venus are considered night planets. They operate to a great extent below the conscious surface. What you can see and what makes sense loses power in the dark. Both the Moon and Venus are motivated by sensations in the body. Less concerned with facts and logic, they live in a world of feelings and experiences, and they both have deep personal needs. But these two are not twins, not even close.

The Moon is completely subjective in its neediness. It just needs what it needs while Venus is always considering and weighing the needs of the "other" and the relationships itself. Venus says, "What about the we?" Moon says, "What about me?" This dance is between the inner emotional child and the desire for relationship. Venus is willing to compromise. The Moon isn't interested in making a deal, but that makes it almost impossible to get what it needs. At some point, most of us start to look beyond childish motivations and attempt to be a partner with someone. How well this goes depends on having a healthy Moon, which means taking care of your inner child and validating your feelings and needs. If you try to do Venus (partnership) while bypassing the Moon, eventually, the bottom will fall out. The most satisfying relationships come from integrating the two: me and we. To do this, you've got to have a solid self to bring to the party. There's just no way around it.

VENUS: RELATIONSHIPS, BALANCE, AND HARMONY

To understand the interaction between the Moon and Venus, let's first explore Venus on its own. We know her as the Roman goddess of love, beauty, art, and sensuality. She's also the Earth goddess and stories tell of flowers sprouting from the ground wherever she stepped. The gods were smitten with Venus and envious of her lovers. Even Mercury, the least inclined toward affairs with immortals, wanted her.

Venus represents desire, love, and attraction. Venus in the birth chart shows what we like, what we find beautiful, and what makes us most open to receiving love and life itself. Beyond romantic and sexual dynamics, Venus rules friendship and companionship. Your Venus, by sign, house, and aspects is not just who and what you're attracted to, but your relationship style; how you do relationships regardless of the people involved. For example, a person with Venus in Scorpio will most likely be emotionally self-protective, somewhat intense and controlling, and want to go deep when it comes to relationships.

In traditional astrology, Venus is also associated with contracts, agreements, music, paintings, fashion, laughter, and good cheer. Venusian type people are often visual artists, musicians, models, interior designers, or drawn to aesthetics. Symmetry, balance, harmony, grace, and diplomacy are all qualities of Venus. Strong Venus comes with a reigning need to keep the peace. The Venus in each of us wants to feel good, be surrounded by beauty, eat delicious food, and entertain the company of lovely and charming people. Venus invites us to indulge in sensual pleasures and taste the sweetness. Life should be easy with Venus, never too hard. Even the Venusian body type is soft, curvy, and dimpled.

Because Venus cares about appearances and judges what's appealing, how things look becomes a bigger deal. When your Venus is active, it's almost unbearable to tolerate what's discordant or ugly to you. The unseemly and uncultured things in life are like hearing fingernails on a chalkboard. You just need that thing entirely removed from your environment.

In evolutionary astrology, Venus also represents essential needs, self-love, and self-worth. What you value most is reflected by Venus. In mythology, Venus never does anything to earn love, she's inherently lovable. Having more money, a better job, or designer clothes won't fill the void if you don't believe in your value, beauty, and worth just as you are. It's not that there's a problem with wanting nice things or working hard to get them, it just doesn't solve an internal self-esteem issue.

Venusian energy is more body than mind. Feeling, touching, being touched, and taking it all in are required to embody this domain. In the tarot, The Empress card corresponds with Venus and she is always depicted pregnant. Venus is the creation of life that comes through union. Union can be through physical intimacy or any partnering. Imagine colors mixing together on a canvas or notes in a song. A couple dancing or a company board meeting. Anytime two or more come together in some form of collaboration, Venus is present.

CYCLES OF THE MOON AND VENUS

We know that the Moon is the fastest mover in our solar system, changing signs every 2.25 to 2.5 days, and completing its cycle every 29.5 days. Venus stays in each sign for about 30 days and completes its orbit around the Sun every 225 days. Venus is much slower moving than the Moon and its rotation is the slowest of all planets in our solar system. It takes Venus 243 Earth days to make one complete revolution on its axis. Venus is also only retrograde 7 percent of the time, the least amount of all planets. All these things considered, we can see Venus as reflecting a more stable, consistent, and grounded aspect of our nature, while the moody Moon is ever-changing in its fluid and whimsical ways.

The relationship between the Moon and Venus is experienced in different ways depending on the individual person, phase of life, or circumstance. Just to be clear before we go any further, we don't believe any planet can be defined as male or female. Everything, including us humans, is made up of masculine/yang *and* feminine/yin energy. There is much written on the Moon as the mother archetype, and we'll touch on it here, but it applies to everyone regardless of gender.

The Moon symbolizes the way we nurture and take care of others, which is linked with our own experience of "mother" or a nurturing parent when we were dependent infants. With the Moon, there's always an underlying need and oftentimes we barter to get those needs met. A child quickly learns what behavior will get them the extra kisses or candy, and the transactions begin. There's a very fine line between mother and baby in the earliest years, and when the baby is in the womb, they're literally in one body.

Venus is the lover archetype. Venus is not motherly affection, the need to protect and care for someone, or the draw to hierarchical love in an attempt to remedy an unfulfilled childhood. Venus is the romance of attracting the object of our desire, just because we want it and to be in relationship with it. In many ways, the Moon represents what we're born into and Venus what we choose for ourselves.

In the natal chart, the personal Moon-Venus birth phase helps us understand our own inner relationship with feelings and needs.

It reflects where we're at in integrating our more subjective, childish Moon needs with our desire to create partnerships and experience love outside of those old family dynamics. The Moon-Venus phase also gives us a good picture of our development in reconciling the needs of me and we. And additionally, we can learn a lot about how our inner mother or nurturing parent is working with our inner lover. You can see how confusion between these two can bring up challenges in relationships. When a romance starts with your inner lover taking the lead, the relationship can take an interesting turn when "mother" suddenly takes over.

The Moon is the brightest body in our night sky and Venus is the second. They both need to be seen, to be loved, and to be fully received. Let's imagine these as the lights that illuminate our inner landscapes, spotlighting what makes our hearts and bodies happy. Ultimately, we feel best when we honor ourselves and our relationships with others. There will always be one beacon of light that is just you (the me), and there is also one for you in partnership (the we). Partnership's not just with other people, it's with life itself.

BRIDGING ME AND WE

Now that we've explored the large playing field of the Moon and Venus, let's get down to how the "me and we" alchemy shows up in the eight phases. When the Moon and Venus come together, the inner emotional self, represented by the Moon, is completely absorbed in the "other" when it comes to relationship. When two planets are conjunct, it's as if they don't even see each other as separate—in this case, the me *is* the we. It's like immersion is happening and the self is being flooded with the other or the other is being flooded with the self. There isn't enough distance between them for much observation or objectivity. As the Moon moves away from Venus, this changes, and it's easier to see the other person as they truly are and to enjoy complementing each other as unique individuals.

When you're studying your Moon-Venus phase, give it time. Pay attention to how you're living and what's happening in your relationships now as well as the patterns you've carried in the past.

The Moon always tends to nurture based on instinct. There's nothing logical about the Moon, but Venus can be rational and realistic. You can determine which planet is taking the lead in your relationships depending on your reactions and demands. If it reminds you of Mom or Dad or it's all about you, it's probably the Moon. If you tend to look to the other first and cooperation and harmony matter more than anything, it's likely Venus.

Venus by nature accepts and passes judgment on others based on what's seen and found appealing. The Moon is always harkening to the past and unconsciously relates everything to emotional experiences and memories that are clung to with the crab's pincers. Venus is more elastic than the Moon and certainly more graceful and approachable. The Moon doesn't mind getting messy. Venus keeps up appearances and expects her partners to do the same. Venus is refined and has no problem with certain rules in relationships. All this "appropriate" and "fair" territory is extremely uncomfortable for the Moon who just wants what it needs and doesn't care about being politically correct. The Moon just needs what it needs, period.

The Venus in each of us is happy to choose. Don't let those Libras, whose ruling planet is Venus, fool you. Even if they avoid making choices because they don't want to rock the boat or look bad, they know what they want. Execution is an entirely different matter. Venus chooses based on liking and disliking, which leads to picking who you want in relationships; who's worth the effort and valuable to you. Compared with the Moon who's driven by instinctual needs, Venus is a bit more conscious and gets down to essential needs, which requires a certain amount of deliberation and weighing of the scales. You might compare these two to an eighteen-month-old baby (Moon) and a twenty-something-year-old adult (Venus).

In relationships, your Moon won't care if something's fair or even makes sense. Your Venus, while also a feeler, will think about things, weighing the outcome and options. Venus compromises and its default is always the "we." Each phase in the Moon-Venus cycle is a step in the evolution of merging our relationship with ourselves with our relationships with the outer world. It's through the mirror of others that we gain more awareness of who we truly are, and the intimacy of seeing another and being seen is at the heart of human desire.

MOON-VENUS PHASES

Your natal Moon-Venus phase is reflected in your relationships, especially with your primary partner(s) or significant others. These dynamics are internal, but we project them outward. In the following phase examples, we're offering some potential external manifestations—how you might feel about and experience your personal relationships.

NEW PHASE (0–45 DEGREES APART) AND THE NEW CONJUNCTION

This phase gives a sense of achievement within that we have found a person with whom we can get along. We usually can't wait to get in touch with each other as there's a strong connection between the two people irrespective of the nature of the relationship. The motivation to get to know each other is greater than ever in the new phase. This often indicates the beginning of a new relationship; however, the following phases determine whether the relationship stands the test of time.

The Moon in a new phase conjunction with Venus is the most personal part of a relationship and it's important for each person to respect the exclusivity of the union. Those with natal Moon-Venus in new phase will likely enjoy a close, personal connection and feel the need for extreme privacy regarding relationship matters. The warmth that's felt between the two people can be quite profound during this period. Usually, inner feelings about the relationship are positive, which might encourage the individual to think about taking things to the next level.

Venus rationalizes the rules that it frames in a person's mind about a relationship. Despite being very satisfied with the well-being of the relationship at this beginning stage, the very nature of Venus brings in a judgmental quality when it comes to needs being met, such as physical security and emotional stability. Both the Moon and Venus are absorbed in feeling, but Venus takes a more logical position. In this phase, there certainly is an expectation of compassion and mutual empathy. The challenge is that there isn't much distance between the "me and we," resulting in very little objectivity. It's easy to lose one's self in the relationship and since Venus is the slower-moving planet, the relationship can almost consume the individual's rhythm represented by the Moon. It's also difficult to see and appreciate the other person for who they are on their own.

During this phase, it's often easy to make the other person feel good, be it a partner, sibling, friend, or family member. Compassion attracts everyone and makes them feel better. We're talking about two personal planets that signify receptivity and it's imperative to understand that this phase highlights the empathic attitude that's usually inherent in all of us to some extent. Moon-Venus new phase people will generally want to establish a comfortable domestic environment, and this attracts others looking for a beautiful, caring place to belong.

CRESCENT PHASE (45–90 DEGREES APART)

During this phase, an individual naturally and consciously takes the initiative and puts in the effort to build a relationship. As the Moon makes a considerable move away from Venus by degrees, it acquires more of the qualities of the sign in which it is placed and starts to distinguish itself outside of Venus' influence. Venus will still hold an overcoming position, but the Moon's independence will have a glimpse here and there.

When the Moon wants something, it really doesn't have a rationale for its needs the way Venus does. Venus rationalizes many relationship-related aspects of life while the Moon has a tendency not to look outside itself to make sense of things. The Moon just goes for what the heart desires when it comes to relationships. In this phase, there can be considerable tension between personal needs and the demands of the relationship or other. With Venus trying to maintain the "we" at all costs, the individual may need to struggle to get enough breathing room to honor and feed their Moon.

In Moon-Venus crescent phase, the individual really wants to find opportunities and chances to connect with the other person, they just aren't sure what it all means yet, or how to do it successfully. The trust factor starts to be existent during this phase as more objective awareness reveals motives and behaviors that could have been missed during the new phase. There's always an indescribable thought in the mind that adds a pinch of reality in terms of the relationship dynamics and the partners themselves. This phase has an earthy nature to it, which motivates the individual to make sure their relationships have the potential to grow into something strong and purposeful. Old patterns threaten progress, but they can be overcome. Overall, there is a growing sense of what is truly needed and what it will take to achieve it.

Venus is a major player when it comes to the principle of satisfaction. Venus is also the part of us that judges the well-being of a relationship. Satisfaction is not just physical satisfaction. This is where we often have some misconception. Venus has a more sensible viewpoint here that includes emotional satisfaction, moral support, and security. In the long run, love, encouragement, and true friendship are the backbone of satisfying relationships. But emotional satisfaction and the sense of having strong moral support develop over a period of time, and in the crescent phase, that level of maturation is often still an idea, not yet fully actualized.

FIRST QUARTER PHASE (90–135 DEGREES APART)

As always, the first quarter phase is an action-oriented, decisive phase in a person's life, especially when it comes to relationships and sexual attraction. There's always heightened physical attraction being felt at various stages of relationships during the Moon-Venus first quarter phase. The relationship may not have completely evolved into something realistic at this point, but satisfaction is measured in terms of the love experienced during time together. Over-attachment to the partner can occur along with possessiveness, even to a dramatic degree. Things may become too much with attitude changes that can be self-centered along with a constant need for attention.

Even though the attraction factor is like a magnet in the first quarter phase, things are much tougher to deal with than in the previous two phases because of a higher degree of emotional involvement. This phase can turn out to be a pivotal stage in life with regards to relationships and the natural outcome. Whether it's perceived as positive or negative is largely dependent on the person and other factors observable in the natal chart. If there are no significant astrological challenges with the Moon or Venus, relationships tend to move forward largely uninterrupted.

With the Moon moving away from Venus, it's difficult to detach from the qualities, emotions, and experiences during the Moon's journey through the zodiac—from the new phase conjunction with Venus to the first quarter phase. By this point, the Moon and Venus have some history together and the Moon is far enough away from Venus to see the past more clearly. There is, however, some conflict in choosing between the Moon's needs and Venus' needs that brings up a whole field of psychological exploration. This is a phase of intense love and serious experiences with partners that often lead to a huge leap toward the next stage of any relationship.

GIBBOUS PHASE (135–180 DEGREES APART)

Gibbous phase has a Virgoan quality and with it comes the compulsion to make things as perfect as possible, all the way down to the fine details. There's a natural ability to know what others need and the dedication and commitment to make relationships work. This can be a very good phase for all matters pertaining to personal satisfaction and happiness because the individual is often willing to do what it takes to make things better.

Most of the expectations out of the relationship are realized during this phase. Before the opposition (full phase), emotions are generally at a very comfortable level, which creates a nice frequency between people. Moon-Venus gibbous phase people are open to listening to other peoples' ideas much more than before. Appreciating each other's thoughts and feelings will strengthen their bond. Friendships usually thrive for those with natal Moon-Venus phase. A sense of togetherness is explicitly felt, and others feel good being around them as they make people feel welcome. Pushing the boundaries to achieve the culmination of "me and we" is what these people focus on. Importantly, the configuration between a soft luminary (Moon) and natural benefic (Venus) imbues the quality of being submissive at times. It tempers the tendency to be overly aggressive or dominating. This is a game-changing quality that gives others a sense of cooperation and belonging.

Venus is still overcoming the Moon in gibbous phase and will impose some of the Venusian values in relationships around things being fair, each person doing their part, and working together in harmony. By this point in the phases, the individual is more conscious about the realistic progress of relationships. There are fewer tendencies to miss cues or over-idealize the other person. This practicality leads to decisions that support personal growth and the evolution of their relationships.

FULL PHASE (180–225 DEGREES APART) AND THE OPPOSITION

Full phase brings awareness, represented by the opposition. At this point in the cycle, the Moon and Venus can see each other with objectivity—like sitting directly across the table. In a relationship, the individual is more ready to accept the other as they are and expects the same in return. This is a phase of reaching maturity when it comes to balancing personal needs with the needs of others and what's best for relationships. The "me and we" may have some push and pull, but the aim is equality. In partnership, there's respect for one another and an effort to complement each other. A similar approach toward society is also exhibited, leading to cooperation, compromise, and effective teamwork.

One of the challenges of full phase is the tendency for projection. This is the phase of the "mirror" and if the individual is not owning the reflection, it's easy to make it about the other person. Unintegrated parts of the self can show up in others or seem like someone else's problems. If the individual fails to realize that every human being is different and expects others to have a similar approach and attitude to their own, the risk of feeling defeated and used is high. There's a longing for reciprocity, but fairness is not always easy to determine when it comes to matters of the heart. Overall, there's plenty of opportunity in this phase to see how the "me" manifests in the "we" and vice-versa. Perhaps for the first time, this phase brings the understanding that polarities are two perspectives or positions in the same field of energy.

Even in a strong relationship with mature individuals, small glitches or inequalities can be overlooked. In an effort to do right by the relationship, appease the other person, and keep things together, personal emotional and childlike needs can be neglected. Over time, individuals in Moon-Venus full phase might come to realize they really can't accept the terms of the relationship. Even though this is a phase of collaboration and integration, there needs to be a reality check because both the Moon and Venus are functioning on their own from their respective positions. Venus tries to rationalize the expectations and progress of the relationship while the Moon is quite aware of what it needs, even if it has no idea how to express it. The key here is in making these two allies and not opponents. One does not have to give up themselves for the other.

DISSEMINATING PHASE (225–270 DEGREES APART)

Now past the opposition, this phase reflects an even greater stage of maturity where the individual is more philosophical about relationships and wants to make a personal contribution to society through partnerships. There's a big shift between the gibbous and disseminating phases because the relationship between the Moon and Venus is considerably different. Before the opposition, Venus was dictating terms to the Moon in some way, but after the Moon passes the opposition point, it starts taking over. In terms of the "me and we," the "me" is stronger and more able to stand on its own and retain its identity in the union of "we." Venus' tendency to rationalize relationships falls behind the power of the Moon's emotional undercurrents.

Expectations of a relationship will often be more focused on emotional satisfaction and security. Emotional needs are also met at an individual level, without the expectation of a partner to make everything okay. A true sign of a mature relationship is an absence of dependency with an active ongoing choice to stay together. This type of relationship is based more on "because I want it" than "because I need it." This same approach is observed with friends and interactions with people in daily life. There is no question of caring or loving—they're both evident. Emotions are quite natural, and in the disseminating phase, the Moon may produce some strong feelings and reactions that Venus can view as upsetting, ugly, or dramatic. But the Moon doesn't care—the heart doesn't play by those rules.

Environment and living conditions can hold a high level of importance during this phase. The individual often attaches to living with someone at a specific place and the spirit of a place matters. The Moon tends to give shape and life to things that didn't appear to be important before. Simple things carry more significance, not because they're necessary to succeed in life, but because they bring happiness and contentment. Vibrations from the surroundings are absorbed readily, so it's important to choose places and people with a positive, high frequency.

LAST QUARTER PHASE (270–315 DEGREES APART)

The last quarter phase is known as a "crisis in consciousness" because of the potential to become aware of what isn't working and what needs to change. When it comes to relationships, this can show up as the sudden realization that what seemed to be working just fine is superficial and inauthentic. The discrepancy between ideals and reality becomes unbearable. Steps need to be taken to live what one believes in. There's a need to accept responsibility for actions that include choices in partners and relationship patterns.

With the Moon moving farther away from Venus, the inner self wants to be seen. If the "me" was previously consumed by the "we" in relationships, there will be a strong drive to individuate and define oneself as an individual.

Venus is certainly not dictating terms here and the Moon holds the upper hand. This means emotions run deeper than usual, but there's a level of honesty with relationships and an ability to see oneself in a greater context. With the Moon farther away from Venus, physical connection increases in importance. Physical touch helps to retain a strong emotional bond during this phase if the people want to stay together. The last quarter phase is about liberating from the past and with both Venus and the Moon being soft planets, some tenderness in the process goes a long way. Change isn't easy and when it hits the most personal parts of who we are and our connections with the people we love, it's even harder. The last quarter phase calls for vision as the entire definition of the "me" and "we" are under revision.

Because of the Moon's agency, another possibility during the Moon-Venus last quarter phase is a sentimental attachment to any person closely associated with the individual. Even though this can be attractive to others in initial relationship stages, it might turn out to be difficult to manage when things get emotional. It's important to be conscious of how others want and need to receive affection, care, and attention—sometimes what seems to be loving is too much or an interruption from someone else's point of view. Being aware of this and respecting boundaries shows respect for others and oneself. It also allows for some healthy space and emotional breathing room.

BALSAMIC PHASE (315–360 DEGREES APART) AND THE BALSAMIC CONJUNCTION

This is a very tricky phase where there's always some kind of secrecy associated with the individual. Extra-relational affairs have a heightened potential to develop. The Moon-Venus balsamic phase indicates an end to specific emotional bondage and physical connection with someone. Whether it will turn out to be the beginning of something else depends upon various factors and signatures in the natal chart. But usually, the new beginning only happens during the new phase conjunction. Individuals may find it difficult to get things going with the right kind of people during this phase. They can also be easily carried away by materialistic desires.

In combination with other challenging signatures in the natal chart, this Moon-Venus phase can lead to addictions and other afflictions that can pull the individual toward a troublesome path in life. On the other hand, balsamic phase can also indicate the ending of a relationship that's been troublesome for a long time. This phase marks the end of tolerance in such relationships and this can be applicable to friendships or even relationships at work. Unrealistic expectations from the other party can be trouble for the individual. During this phase, they're probably reaching the point of being "done" with keeping up with these expectations and an end is clearly signified, at least at a psychological level. Difficult emotions are almost always involved.

The Moon-Venus balsamic phase also involves maintaining a low profile in various situations. The need for emotional connection is felt at an inner level. The drive to care for one's self is always present during this phase but caring and compassion for loved ones is also a clear focus. Many things will appear to be in the dark, and emotional relationship issues buried beneath the surface can be looked into deeply to get them sorted out. The Moon's dominance in this phase will suggest that matters appear to be of self-interest, without making much sense to others, but are purely in the best interest of the betterment of relationships.

Meditating on how to take things forward with a better balance of "me and we" is a challenge, but it needs to be achieved. Reaching the end of one cycle always indicates we're continuously looking out for what's next. It's not that whatever one has at this point in terms of relationship and emotions will end. It is, however, a period of strong energy where a great deal of introspection goes into finding out the answers to various questions related to "me and we." At the end of the cycle, we're constantly in preparation for the future. We're determined to make sure that things will be good in whatever chapter comes next. At the end of the day, each phase is an experience in life. This final phase puts us in the path of constant transition, where we're always on the lookout for something better, always with the "we" in heart and mind.

FIVE

The Moon and Mars: Bridging Reaction and Action

In spiritual practice, there's much emphasis on the higher mind, higher realms, and higher chakras. Astrologically speaking, that usually means Jupiter, Uranus, and Neptune. The fullest actualization of our selves includes these higher aspects—but this fulfillment won't happen without the lower mind, lower realms, and lower chakras. And higher is not better than lower.

When we embody our Moon and Mars in their healthiest expressions, we become emotionally stable, comfortable in our bodies, and able to respond to anything life throws at us. We act on our own behalf and meet our own needs. A strong sense of self and plenty of energy to keep us going are vital to everything we do. In a basic sense, it all begins with the Moon and Mars, and if that foundation isn't sound, it won't matter how high we try to climb. When the bottom or roots can't hold, eventually it all comes down. Your Moon-Mars relationship is worth your attention. And if you're interested in following your heart's desire, Neptune isn't going to swoop in and take you there. It's through your Moon (Heart) and Mars (Desire) that you not just find it but live it.

A LITTLE MOON-MARS STORY

In a typical Indian village, marriages still happen in a very traditional and orthodox manner where the parents of the bride and the groom search for a perfect match for their children by consulting all the elders of the family. Once the pre-talks are complete, the parents exchange the couple's horoscopes. Yes, confirming astrological synastry is of primary importance in India before marriage. An astrologer checks the charts of the soon-to-be-married couple and concludes if their married life will be blissful. If either of the families (bride's or groom's) don't feel satisfied with the astrologer's conclusion, the case is closed (the marriage is a no-go) and both families begin their search again—back to square one!

Let's look at the following example. A boy falls head over heels for a boy and the boy also feels the same about him. If they get into a relationship without objectively considering compatibility, such as seeking the advice of an astrologer (wink), there's much less chance that the marriage will go smoothly. It's likely they'll get separated or even divorced. We only need to look at the divorce rate in the United States to prove our point. We don't want to digress into reasons for successful marriages or arguments for *any* relationship do's or don'ts—that's beyond the scope of this book. But we need something to play around with, so on we go. Let's consider that our couple wants to marry and they're ready to solve any problems, but the parents are doing their best to separate them because of various cultural reasons. So where do the Moon and Mars show up here?

The couple wants to get married no matter what. This is the Moon side of the couple. They don't want to sacrifice their togetherness for anyone's sake. They're pretty darn stubborn. This is a strong Moon trait as the Moon limits our vision and makes us visualize only what we want without giving much thought to other conditions that might influence the situation. The couple has grit and their ability to face the consequences of their choice to live a life together is a Martial trait. Their ability to stick to their agenda and face their problems without giving in to the feelings or disapproval of others is the combined quality of the Moon and Mars. Whether it works out in the long run, it's a victory in the realm of independence and emotional security. They've taken a risk to leave the past behind and follow their hearts, and they're doing it together.

The parents, on the other hand, want to stop the couple and choose who their children will marry. They want to follow the customs and procedures of their respective families. A great deal of pride lies here. To the parents, their self-respect is at stake. The fear of losing respect in society is a real concern. They want to maintain their self-respect and they won't part with it at any cost, which is a stubborn Moon quality. This is also egoistic, and the Moon represents the human ego. The idea of sticking selfishly to what we want (ego) can overtake us. We exhibit this behavior time and again in various situations throughout our lives. As self-aware as we might think we are, it's often others who notice our self-absorbed and selfish behavior, while we remain oblivious. The actions the parents might take to stop the couple from getting married are Martial in nature because they're backed by a specific need of a specific scenario, and their actions are influenced by what they want. With both the couple and parents, we can see how personal wants and needs drive the show. And that's the way of Moon-Mars.

MARS: INITIATION AND AUTHENTIC DESIRE

Mars is the last of the inner planets after the Moon, Sun, Mercury, and Venus. Even in the solar system, Mars is placed in an interesting middle ground—being a transition point from inner planets to outer planets from a geocentric point of view. Mars is ready to look ahead and march forward. Mars provides us the courage to look beyond our comfort zone. Mars brings in the quality of individuality in a human being even though they might be forced to follow orders at times. Mars helps us express ourselves in a temperamental standpoint in extreme situations. Mars represents our initiative and our guts.

Desiring with self-assertion to reach a goal on a specific path is the classic Martial trait that drives our lives forward. Acting upon something with assertion is a quality that Mars instills within us. Mars signifies the active traits in human beings, or the human doing. The glyph of Mars is a small circle with the base of an arrow connected to the outside edge of the circle. The arrow is coming out of the circle, symbolizing breaking out of containment, like a baby leaving the womb. It directly indicates moving ahead in a direction to do something. Mars is a planet of separation. Its manifestations are not always the stories we cheer about. Anger, impatience, failure to think first, and lust are just some of the costumes Mars wears. But we all need to pursue our passions, live our own lives, and do our thing. Mars helps us get up and go and stand up for ourselves. And Martial experiences can be the most effective in teaching us some quick lessons about life and ourselves.

CYCLES OF THE MOON AND MARS

Mars takes 686 Earth days to complete one revolution around the Sun. If in normal motion, it takes about 45 days to transit through one sign of the zodiac. Mars retrograde is not a common phenomenon and the percentage of Mars retrograde birth charts is as low as 7 to 10 percent. Mars turns retrograde the least frequently of all planets. This is very fitting for the planet of action and moving forward.

By the time Mars transits through one sign of the zodiac, the Moon will finish a full and a half lunations. During this time, human moods and feelings go through various influences and we experience emotions such as happiness, sadness, disgust, fear, surprise, and anger at different degrees or intensities. Stabilizing the emotions and maintaining a clear mindset to approach the immediate aspect of life with the right balance of action and reaction is the challenge. The Moon is only halfway through a lunation cycle when Mars moves into the next sign, meaning Mars makes a move into new territory before the Moon has completed its cycle. Change is threatening to the Moon. Metaphorically, this shows how Mars is the one changing the game, going ahead while the Moon is still trying to finish. In working with the Moon-Mars phases, we're learning about these forces in ourselves and how they can work against and with each other.

The Moon's journey through the signs of the zodiac builds up the action with multiple influences, which we all exhibit as reactions in real-life situations. Action continues while it keeps being modified by the different experiences we have as time passes by. All these experiences result in reaction, which eventually has an effect on our action. This is a cycle that can be better understood in terms of bridging the Moon and Mars.

BRIDGING REACTION AND ACTION

With the Moon and Mars, we're talking about a sensitive side and a hardcore side of human beings. We're dealing with what we feel and what we do. Basically, what we feel is what we do, which is action. And how we feel about what we've done is reaction. Reaction is not just in response to what we've done or what we're doing. It's basically our answer, or response, to an action. Every action has its own reaction. From this view, we're looking at the Moon as reaction and Mars as action. If we think about it, almost our entire lives are spent based on action and reaction, which means the Moon and Mars are an inseparable and integral point of human evolution. The commonalities between Venus and the Moon are more in line because they have similar traits. However, the beauty of the Moon and Mars is how they co-exist despite their contrasting natures. Life lies in the difference and that is where the Moon and Mars thrive. Looking closely, we'll find that every situation in our lives is alive with the Moon and Mars.

Mars is energy; however, the Moon is the catalyst for that energy. It might sound absurd to consider the Moon as a catalyst of energy when energy is a primary Martial trait, but let's go further. The Moon is reaction and Mars is action. We all act based upon something and that something can be anything. But the mindset to act is the Moon's territory. The Moon picks up the motivation of Mars and metaphorically lights up the stove, putting that fire into action! So any given scenario is first felt at an inner level by the Moon. The position of the Moon in the natal chart is clearly indicative of how a person perceives and reacts to scenarios in life. For example, there's a world of difference between the Moon in Aries and the Moon in Scorpio. The Moon in Aries gives an impulsive and nervous feeling that doesn't lessen its dominating attitude. Aries Moon people can be extremely effective when challenged by something. They're open to accepting challenges but with a clear mindset. Contrastingly, Moon in Scorpio people can harbor insecurities and fear a loss of control. These individuals are quite sensitive and always wage a battle to balance between the extremes—be it love or hate. The intensity of feelings with Scorpio Moon people is quite high.

Individual reactions to specific life scenarios vary, as reflected by the Moon's signature in the birth chart. Actions will be based upon what the Moon dictates psychologically, based on the natal position. Likewise, action (Mars) also gets modified. A person with Mars in Cancer (ruled by the Moon) can have an unpredictable temper and might have a history of acting aggressively in unexpected and unwanted circumstances. Yes, *unwanted* circumstances. When fiery Mars is placed in an emotional spectrum, like Cancer, the individual may find it difficult to navigate the tides of feelings, needs, emotions, and comfort. Mars wants to get on the field and kick the ball through the goal posts. It's not a Martial quality to wait there, but Cancer is cautious and rarely heads toward anything directly. As a result, such a person's actions might manifest in other ways that could be a waste of energy. It can be a great challenge for Mars in Cancer individuals to channel their energy in the best path. They tend to wait or retreat when it really is go-time and overdo things that just don't require that much effort.

We all have our unique flavor. Understanding how you work and are wired helps you make better use of your own energy. Balancing actions and reactions based on the relationship between the Moon and Mars will give you a more detailed vision to understand the intricacies of accepting the mixture of action and reaction in your life.

MOON-MARS PHASES

There's an amorphous quality to the Moon-Mars cycle. Maybe that's why you'll find so much written about these phases—we're providing ideas about something that's better grasped through feeling and experience.

NEW PHASE (0–45 DEGREES APART) AND THE NEW CONJUNCTION

Any new phase conjunction between planets is like two parts of yourself getting together or having a conversation for the first time. The word "new" suggests something that hasn't happened before, at least in the way it's happening now. When the Moon, the part of us most deeply attached to safety, history, and emotional needs, meets erratic and pushy Mars, there's going to be a fight somewhere. The Moon wants to belong. What happens when its arm is linked with Mars who desires nothing more than to break free and make its own way? Mars as an archetype is separation. The Moon is traditionally associated with the mother goddesses and the mystery from which we all come. As a water planet/luminary, the Moon naturally wants to homogenize or unify things. It relates through sameness and looks for similarities between itself and others. Mars is a fiery planet, consumed with the need to develop its own identity. Fire by nature is competitive and challenging. It wants to be different and celebrates differences. In this phase, the old self-identity we've become attached to must find new roots in a new direction.

Mars, as the slower-moving planet, holds more ground, at least at first. Mars is pushing the Moon to do something different, and the Moon instinctually receives this as an attack. It's common for Moon-Mars new phase individuals to hold a great deal of anger within and toward themselves. With the Moon ruling the stomach and digestion, this can show up as ulcers and tummy issues of all kinds. Everything with the Moon links back to the emotions, so angry feelings, upsetting memories, emotional eating, and heightened reactivity are par for the course. It's easy to label these things "bad," but Mars is just using its powers to get things moving. Sometimes it takes a lot to get the Moon out of its comfort zone, and Mars doesn't like taking no for an answer.

Individuals in this phase are emotionally charged. Any planets in conjunction seem to operate as one, meaning it's difficult to distinguish between the two. Using the Moon and Mars as our example here, the individual may not be aware of when they're reacting versus initiating in a proactive way. Both the Moon and Mars are defensive, but for different reasons. The Moon is a protector of what is known, keeping things the same. Mars protects independence and one's calling to do what it takes to achieve a greater purpose. In a domestic setting, Mars shows up as the teenager who wants out of the house and as the Moon when something goes wrong and they want to run back home. The Moon-Mars new phase is a signature of empowering the self to take a risk and go its own way. It will take every bit of Mars' courage, strength, and unstoppable forward-motion to turn the tide of the past, and the biggest battle these individuals will face is with themselves.

CRESCENT PHASE (45–90 DEGREES APART)

A new course is underway now, but not much distance has been covered. Mars is still exercising force to keep up the momentum; it would be easy to fall back into the old ways. Crescent phase is uncomfortable because there's a struggle with the past that can seem relentless. Taurean energy infuses this phase and is perhaps the most difficult sign to move when it digs in and stands its ground.

While the individual is moving, it's slow and laborious and it will still be a while before results are obvious. New habits and patterns only establish when they've been done enough times to become part of the routine. The Moon seduces with memories and emotional comfort, whispering, "Come back and everything will be okay." Mars wants the Moon to see the value in going forward, but it's hard to convince the Moon without time-tested proof. Mars wants action motivated by its own spontaneous and authentic desire. This phase is about choosing to act in alignment with the heart's true calling, even when it feels against the grain.

It's critical that Moon-Mars crescent phase individuals keep putting one foot in front of the other. When triggers and troubles show up, reacting is normal, but there's a strong need to keep one's sights on where they're going and not fall into traps of the past. Consider how often reactions get results. Take for example a child who reacts by screaming to a parent who doesn't give a treat on-demand. The parent may not be able to take the piercing, dramatic reaction, especially in public, and gives the child the treat. Reactions are powerful and we've all learned how to make them work for us, manipulating things to get what we want and need. Moving from a reactive to active life approach doesn't happen overnight. The "what I need" can trump "what I want," especially when we don't feel emotionally stable. Mars challenges the Moon to redefine security so we can do more and go further.

Crescent phase is similar to Mars cracking the whip and kicking a horse that could just as easily drop to the ground as well as keep up the pace. The horse, or the Moon, needs to feel taken care of and to trust the rider with its life. These individuals are learning to prove to themselves that they can safely go after what they want and grow beyond what they've known themselves to be. Both the Moon and Mars correspond with physicality. They reflect our human bodies and energy, so it's common for those in this phase to experience physical tiredness. Mars reflects the quality of our life force and our "get-up-and-go." With the intense resistance created in this phase, it's unusual not to experience its effects in the body. Getting plenty of exercise boosts vitality and mood and is key to energetically keeping the flow going in the newly established direction.

FIRST QUARTER PHASE (90–135 DEGREES APART)

With more distance between the Moon and Mars, the first quarter phase allows a greater perspective when it comes to actualizing the self and personal desires. It's not clear yet, but things are starting to come together. Individuals may push their agendas forward passionately without much prior thought or planning. This phase is known for its activity, and growth comes through testing things out to see what happens. With the Moon and Mars, the struggle for driving the personal agenda reaches a new level, with the Moon finally getting some space of its own—the past does have its value after all. The first quarter phase begins at 90 degrees, with the square aspect, and in fact, Moon and Mars are squaring off here. They're in a relationship of constant challenge, and the only way to work things out is by going at it! This is a classic example of "Should I stay, or should I go?" where you try one or the other or combinations of both depending on the situation.

Mars and the Moon are both associated with ego. To clarify here, ego is not something to transcend or dissolve. Ego is what makes each of us unique individuals with talents and gifts that allow us to serve our purpose. In some ways, this phase is the forging of the past definition of self and the one that's currently emerging. Whichever direction the ship's going, it's picked up enough speed to be a force to be reckoned with. The individual wants to show others what they're doing and how they're admirable and brave. Awareness from the new through gibbous phases (just like Aries through Virgo) is subjective, meaning we see things and people from our inner reality. Subjective awareness is all about experiencing external things through our internal filter, like how others are affecting us and how we feel about them. With the Leonine essence of this phase and lack of objectivity, it's easy to demand feedback and approval from the outside world. Individuals in this phase often do not own the unsuccessful and sometimes disastrous results of their efforts. It's so easy to take everything personally, feeling that life is doing things *to* them or failing to support them.

It may not sound like it, but this phase isn't any less positive than the others. Anytime we act and show off our stuff, we're more likely to get attention, and from action comes reaction. The first quarter phase is naturally super creative, passionate, and expressive. With the Moon and Mars in this dance or dynamic, there's ample opportunity for emotional creativity if one is so inclined. The challenge in this phase is exactly what ignites the creative fire. Leadership qualities can also emerge here along with a new license on life that can inspire oneself and others to do great things with wholehearted joy. If Mars can keep proving to the Moon that its fire won't burn the whole house down, the show can move farther down the road.

GIBBOUS PHASE (135–180 DEGREES APART)

Gibbous phase is a period of adjustments and fine-tuning. It's the last step before full phase, the fulfillment or completion of what's been growing throughout the entire waxing, or building, half of the cycle. Anything that isn't working, that's not just right, or even slightly "off" will need to be examined and picked apart to make it better. At this point in the Moon-Mars journey, it's possible to reach a crisis point. This is especially true if the individual hasn't found a constructive way to create more personal agency and proactively take charge of their life. Moon-Mars is a cycle of learning to fight for oneself, in the most positive ways. If there's been a tendency to fall back into old reaction patterns at the expense of following a true prompting to be and do things differently, this is the phase where it feels like you're being zipped into a suit that's five sizes too small. We all need to grow, and growth comes through the uncomfortable, awkward, and unknown territory. On the other hand, the individual may realize they've been overly arrogant and inauthentic in attempts to blaze their own trail. Whether the mark was shot too high or low, this is the call to get it perfect. Not perfect as in free of errors, but perfect as in perfectly suited to one's self.

A keyword for this phase is "overcoming." Gibbous phase reflects the overcoming of yourself (self with a lowercase s). Overcoming doesn't mean leaving it behind, it means gaining some mastery over it. This entire chapter on reaction versus action and belonging versus breaking away of the Moon and Mars is about discovering that our past isn't separate from our present or future. We break things down in life, especially in gibbous phase, to try and understand them, change them, and/or fix them, but it's never about the "things." It's our perspective that needs shifting and tweaking. There's a way to alchemize what we understand and how we identify with our past (the Moon) and how we're driven with raw willpower to make something new with/of ourselves (Mars). Whether individuals in this phase are conscious of it, that's what they're doing. And this will determine what version of the alchemized self will emerge in the following full phase to be seen and used to give oneself to the world and life itself.

Even though Mars can be self-centric, it wants more than just the gratification of personal desires. Mars needs to serve something greater. Mars needs something to fight for and an honorable purpose worthy of its dedication. In this phase, individuals spend time in self-analysis, which leads to self-improvement. This is important because what the hero Mars is looking for is the self. "Would I follow myself into battle?" is a good question to pose here. Most of us, including animals, follow those who are confident in where they're going and act from a place of integrity. Think of this phase as a dress rehearsal or final editing. Does everything line up? More specifically, is your mind, heart, and action in alignment? This is the time to face feelings of inadequacy and choose self-love. Being the best we can be is a sacred art and the gibbous phase embodies its essence.

FULL PHASE (180–225 DEGREES APART) AND THE OPPOSITION

Any cycle or planetary relationship in this stage indicates the full light of awareness, the same way the full moon shines down, illuminating the night. What was previously, at least partially, developing in the dark is now out for everyone to see. Moon-Mars full phase has much to do with finally seeing ourselves for what we are and becoming aware of how we project our personal selves into the world.

Whether they realize it or not, individuals in this phase have found a way to take their past, more conditioned sense of self and integrate it with their current unfolding individualized self. They're becoming aware of the dynamic tension between the two in an objective way and have more-or-less settled on an alchemy of the two as the path forward. What does this look like? It could be someone who becomes clear about how the past has been impacting their behavior and decisions and consciously projects a new self into the world. Or it could be someone who battles between the Moon's need for belonging and safety and Mars' charge toward independence and excitement. The opposition at 180 degrees can feel like a tug-of-war and all of full phase carries that push and pull. The individual's state of consciousness determines how they will manifest this energy. Just because something is visible doesn't mean we'll choose to see it and own it, but in this phase that opportunity is present.

The nature of full phase is revealing, interactive, and social. Because the Moon and Mars are both self-focused and instinctual, this doesn't automatically result in an extroverted conversationalist, but the individual will look to the external world to find balance within themselves. In this chapter, we talked about the Moon as reaction and Mars as action. To clarify, when triggered, both the Moon and Mars can be very reactive, but the pure heart of Mars is initiating action directly toward its goal or object of desire. The Moon is receptive, soft, cool, and wet. Mars is assertive, hard, hot, and dry. Individuals in this phase are trying to balance and integrate these contrasting parts of themselves, but it's often easier to project the more difficult of the two. Depending on the rest of the chart and how the person is actualizing their potential, they could identify more easily with the Mars impulse and project the Moon onto others or the converse scenario, owning the Moon and projecting Mars. When it's hard to get opposing parts to work together harmoniously, it's natural to want to push one out of the picture or expect someone else to meet those needs.

Oppositions and full phase signatures in the natal chart point to major life themes and more than any other aspect or phase draw experiences from the external world to get our attention. Individuals with Moon-Mars in this phase can expect to interact with others to re-enact their own early childhood and teenager dynamics in some form or another. It could be that as they're putting themselves out there, pursuing the path of their calling, someone shows up with extreme resistance and does everything they can to keep the individual "home" or in an emotional Moon-like symbiotic containment. In its movement, the Moon has gained more ground, being across from Mars, and if the lunar-self hasn't been effectively integrated by this point, it will hold its ground until given an equal seat at the table. Hiding is not a viable option in full phase. The person has developed a strategy for moving forward as an individual, in pursuit of desires and meeting personal needs; to reconcile its reactions to the past and actions for creating a new present.

The ego-self has reached a new level of maturation and now the individual must run with it or not. We know that turning eighteen years old doesn't mean we're all grown up, and the full phase can feel this way, sometimes unprepared for reality. There can be profound moments of realizing "this is what I'm working with" and "this is how it really is," with vast opportunities to get the balance right and put oneself to good use. This can be a powerful cycle of self-actualization in the world with an understanding and deepening of relationships. The ability to learn about oneself through others and genuinely appreciate others in their own unique cycles is a blessing to everyone.

DISSEMINATING PHASE (225–270 DEGREES APART)

Now that the integrated personal self is out there, for better or worse, it's time to find out how to best contribute to society. What can be done with the self, within the rules, structures, and limits of life as we know it? The preceding period of getting ready, developing, and then becoming aware of personal potential in a greater context has concluded. It's go-time in the world. The disseminating phase has a Capricornian flavor that motivates the individual to climb the ladder, achieve goals, and earn respect. They will generally work hard to make use of their past and honor history (Moon) while applying their willpower (Mars) to move forward in life. They can be particularly good at seeing the bigger picture and "playing the game," especially at work, which often paves the way to success.

The disseminating phase is the mountaintop of the entire cycle and during this period of development, the individual will hit a ceiling. When it comes to Moon-Mars, part of that "ceiling" is the personal or ego sense of self. We can do only so much to shape ourselves, but eventually, that ends, and we work with what is, almost like someone reaching seventy-five years. Not that we can't shift and change in all stages, but seventy-five is a completely different perspective and experience from seven or twenty-seven, or even fifty-seven. There's a harshness to this time because growth has reached its maximum point and there's a responsibility to demonstrate its meaningfulness and usefulness. All wisdom accumulated up to now is meant to be shared more broadly, with less personal attachment.

Most of us know what Saturn feels like and if you tune into that vibration, you get a feel for this phase. Now imagine Moon-Mars under Saturn's direction and you'll get what we mean. Everything the individual has worked through—past and present, struggles with family and emotions, the need to belong and the impulse to do their own thing, in their way, all nearly freezes in time. Its crystallization is necessary, so that we stop fidgeting and take accountability for it. If something's always moving or changing it's hard to determine where it fits. These self-imposed brakes in the evolution of lowercase "s" self halt the process and give the individual time to face their conditioned responses, which by this point will likely be breaking down. One of the best things about hitting a limit or boundary is that we can feel whether the direction we've been going is authentic or not. We might not be able to change it now, just like a law in our current government, but we're building strength in the knowledge of what works and what doesn't. If something's off, we can own it, even if rebuilding isn't possible at this time. The next round of anything we enter will be supported with this maturity that only comes through age and experience.

Individuals in the Moon-Mars disseminating phase possess the ability to apply their emotional and physical innate instincts toward a collective vision. Their timing is usually good, reflexes sharp, and intuition keen. With a strategic quality, they can sense what a group, company, or nation needs and practically rearrange things for better efficiency and results. They also recognize where they personally fit in the picture and can make it their mission to carry out that role with a remarkable sense of duty. It's important to note that it's easy to get lost in the realm of expectations and preconceived ideas of success at this point, and even more so, easy to feel superior when meeting material standards of achievement. The goal here is to bring the wisdom of the past and present and the vision for the future into alignment in ways that stabilize and sustain our civilization. The personal mission must fold into a greater mission or else be sacrificed. In this phase, there isn't room for selfish ambition. If the individual runs in that direction, they might initially be rewarded, but eventually, karma and the boundaries of collective society will close that door. The wise ones catch themselves in excessive self-righteousness and domination before the external walls constrict to confine them within. In this phase, there is truth to the old saying "play or be played," and breaking through the illusions around both is part of the process.

LAST QUARTER PHASE (270–315 DEGREES APART)

The Moon-Mars last quarter phase is associated with a reorientation of the most personal, instinctual self. Wherever the individual has ended up in the dance between hanging onto the past and forging into new territory, they're up for a final assessment. This is less to do with changing the outcome and more to do with the awareness and understanding of how and why they've done the things they're done and become the person they've become. This is a crisis in consciousness, like all last quarter phase signatures. And there's still hope for progress, especially if the individual can step back and observe themselves without the obstruction of excessive emotional attachment. It never does any good to judge the past based on what you know and who you are now. The last quarter phase is infused with Aquarian energy and offers the benefit of spending a little time on the outside looking in, so personal obstacles can be transcended, and the self can be understood from a new, inspired perspective.

Perhaps the greatest gift of this phase (there are many and ranking is subjective) is in offering oneself as an example for others to learn from. This involves candid sharing and a willingness to let the story serve others in the way best suited to them. The self is the example here, and it's possibly something to be proud of and worthy of emulating. However, it's equally likely that the individual's self-example is filled with a rocky road of choices and consequences that aren't traditionally considered admirable. Maybe they failed to live up to their potential or pursued a path of destructive or dishonest behavior. Maybe they didn't do anything particularly dreadful, but never moved past the comfort zone of predictability, feeding into insecurities. At this point, the heroic action is to let their path, whatever it may be, shine a light for others and their future selves. There is equal opportunity for growth from all angles when there is awareness and a commitment to work with what *is* for the betterment of humankind. The "what is" we're referring to *is* the individual.

If Moon-Mars is the integration of reaction and action, belonging and breaking out, the past and present sense of self, here's where the cards are called. The best question the individual can ask and do their best to not just answer but actualize, is, "What more can I do with my personal life before it starts to fade away?" You might notice we have less to say at this point than in previous phases and that's fitting for the territory. Perhaps someone at this point in the journey might feel this way about it: I did it this way. I might not do it this way were I to start it all now, but that holds nothing worth pursuing. And what I did (Moon) will always shape what I do (Mars). So I will do my best to consciously understand the past for the sole purpose of creating a better future.

BALSAMIC PHASE (315–360 DEGREES APART) AND THE BALSAMIC CONJUNCTION

The impulse of Mars is to create life. The impulse of the Moon is to protect life. The balsamic phase is a time for dying, putting them both on guard. Negotiations between the Moon and Mars lose significance in the context of the bigger picture. The personal process of integrating needs and wants, bridging reaction with action, honoring the need to belong and "get the hell out of town"—all the things we've been talking about up until this point cease to matter. For individuals in Moon-Mars balsamic phase, their very identity can feel like it's receding into the blur. Even through moments of emotional reactivity, there's a sense of fate or destiny settling in. It's something akin to the expression, "Wherever you go, there you are." At the end of the cycle, there's very little to do, although the individual might convince themselves otherwise, at least for a while.

The impulse to fight for what one is and defend who they've known themselves to be loses its potency. This isn't giving up in any negative sense of the words. It's giving up the very definition and attachments to the idea of self. The closer the individual is to the balsamic conjunction, the stronger the need to withdraw from the external world to listen to their internal voice. Wisdom comes from introspection and contemplation. The past and present have merged. The form will certainly vary from person to person—some more tied to the past and where they come from, some more engaged with their individual freedom to create something new.

The personal self has developed as far as it will in this cycle. The most supportive thing anyone can do in the balsamic phase is to let go of what was and create spaciousness for what will be. This is a transition point and like any major life change, there's a range of emotions to experience. Sadness and grief are common because something is being left behind, and in this case, it's the sense of self. Even the nature of vitality and life itself can seem distorted in this phase. Reality bends and one's face, body, and human functions can seem surreal. Both the Moon and Mars are experienced in part through the physical body, leaving the individual to face themselves as if in a carnival's house of mirrors. Aging itself will awaken new awareness. Part of their path is surrendering the ego definition of self, including appearance, for a more spiritual or energetic experience of their essence.

We wouldn't be writing about balsamic phase if the game was entirely over. Endings feed beginnings and meaningful closure is an art. These individuals have the mission of clearing, preparing, and feeding the next cycle. With Moon-Mars, that will require sacrificing something of themselves. It's impossible to define this generally. Everyone has different attachments and tethers that keep them repeating old history. Those attachments and tethers, whatever they may be, are what need to be faced, loved, and released with gratitude. The person in this phase wouldn't be where they are now without those things—it was all part of the path. Sometimes we talk about getting on the path or finding our path, but there is nowhere to be except your path; you're on it and you can't fall off it or get off it. The individual in this phase has the potential to see its entirety; to see their journey on the spiral of evolution from beginning to end, which is just another beginning.

This phase is rich in the potential for accepting oneself and one's interconnectedness with everything else, which means it's equally ripe for denial, hopelessness, and isolation. As the motivation for personal and material success wanes, the urge to contribute to society increases. What this really means is that the individual has chosen this lifetime to deconstruct their world in the ways they've related to it. As old baggage is left behind, true treasures are discovered and passed forward. In offering the best of oneself for the future, profound peace, forgiveness, faith, and understanding can arise. The balsamic phase embodies Piscean energy, which is vast and represents the great unknown. If one embraces that mystery within and without, the transition, even with its trials, will be magical. If they cling to the past, too afraid they'll be lost in a void, suffering and loneliness can be consuming. On this planet, there's no escape from endings. And they are one of the most honest tests of character and courage.

SIX
The Moon and Jupiter: Bridging Inner and Greater Consciousness

The planetary cycles teach lessons to human beings and the cycles are basically various levels of human experiences. The Moon-Jupiter cycle is all about bridging the gap between our own inner thoughts and the thoughts that occupy our minds during the course of higher learning in our lives. We all have some level of spiritual inclination inside us; there is no person in this world without it—it just means something different to each of us.

FOR THE GOOD OF SELF AND HUMANITY

In this cycle where the Moon is released from Jupiter, we see that the Moon leaves Jupiter when there is a nice blend of an inner and greater consciousness, which is the state of innocence. As and when we grow, we gain experiences in life that influence the further course of our bridging inner and greater consciousness. This is where we tend to lose sight of the greater thoughts when we think about our own selves. Our human proximity to the material world blinds us to spiritual ideas and through this Moon-Jupiter cycle, we learn the lesson of being practical in terms of achieving our material needs to survive in today's world without giving up the greater cause for which we were actually born. As this is a cycle, we fall back to the same initial idea of "innocence," which is a culmination of the inner consciousness and greater consciousness.

In this modern world, the availability of literary sources is abundant, and we all have different understandings of the same concept. This is applicable to the idea of consciousness as well. Different religious scriptures say different things about consciousness. A psychological approach towards astrology gives its own way of perceiving consciousness. Astrologically, without the Moon, there is no being. When there is no being, there is no consciousness.

Consciousness can be seen as the actual being of a person at that particular moment and time. Each of us is influenced by various factors in life and they are always multiple because we all come from different families, cultures, and demographics, and whatever is available to us forms our physical and mental being. Our mental being is termed as the "consciousness." We all have the moonish side within us that is usually selfish (not in a negative way) because we're all bound by our needs and desires, which often becomes the driving force of our lives. This is what we call the "inner consciousness"—the exploration of our inner mind as to what we need and what we perceive of things that are available to us in order to lead our lives.

On the other hand, we all certainly have the greater self inside us that thinks about things that don't necessarily concern us personally but are universally important. We often don't realize that our spiritual well-being is not just for our own sake but also for our community. Our spiritual well-being has a direct influence on the people with whom we live and encounter in our daily lives. This is the side of us that's generous in sharing our intellectual or spiritual resources with others for a greater good, which always constitutes a community, society, city, or even a nation. Indian emperor Ashoka the Great felt a great deal of sorrow and disdain when he witnessed the bloodshed during the war of Kalinga in the third century BCE, and it made him give up his will to conquer. His softened approach enabled him to propagate a new ideology, which eventually became a new religion called Buddhism.

GENEROUS JUPITER

Traditionally a natural benefic planet, Jupiter is often associated with progeny, prosperity, justice, temples, spirituality, religion, philosophy, rank, honor, income, and well-being. Jupiter is one of the ministers of the King's Court who gives advice to the King in terms of the economy and well-being of the kingdom. Jupiter is a go-to planet for astrologers as we commonly look for Jupiter aspects that can reduce the ill effects of a challenging placement of another planet to a large extent.

Jupiter is the true indicator of the righteousness inside us, which leads to the destiny of our spiritual or greater life embedded within the greater consciousness. Jupiter also relates to most things we consider to be good or positive, which makes it easier for us to accept the matters taught by Jupiter, while we find it harder to accept and receive teachings when it comes to Saturn. Jupiter is closer to the luminaries than Saturn and a planet's relative speed and distance is a matter of differentiation. Saturn is also colder and hence perceived as harder. Basically, Jupiter just feels more accommodating, approachable, and just like its name Jove is jovial. Jupiter reminds us not to underestimate ourselves. It instills confidence, expands our consciousness, and affirms that we're capable of being and doing more than we've ever been or done before.

Jupiter makes us think beyond a tangible material life with a greater sense of compassion and comradery. This doesn't mean Venusian compassion for those closest to us. It's the kind of compassion in offering a person we don't know, who hasn't had food for two days, a meal. Jupiter reiterates the greater meaning of why we're here and inspires us to take the high road. Jupiter is our path and our truth. It holds the purpose of our incarnation, and we, in some way, are destined to be what we are!

CYCLES OF THE MOON AND JUPITER

Jupiter takes about 12 months to move from one sign to the next. This is almost a perfect astronomical sync that beautifully turns out to be a yearly cycle. And that cycle gives a lot of symbolic as well as archetypal meaning to human life. The Moon forms twelve conjunctions with Jupiter in a year and as the Moon travels, it picks up the basic qualities and energies of all the signs and planets. For example, while Jupiter transits Scorpio, the Moon will enter Scorpio and conjunct Jupiter every month that year, continuing on through the remaining signs after each conjunction until the two meet again. Symbolically, this can represent twelve different topics based upon the sign in which the Moon is posited, which is similar to the twelve houses concept. The Moon is continually working through the twelve archetypes as it's always moving through them. As the Moon meets Jupiter in Scorpio these twelve times over a year, it's working through them all within the Scorpio Jupiter context. Twelve is a very important number in astrology. There are twelve signs in the zodiac and twelve astrological houses. Symbolically, we can associate each phase of the Moon with respect to Jupiter's position in the zodiac with each of the twelve areas of human development. The bridging of our inner and greater consciousness can be seen as carrying the same theme and meaning as the twelve houses.

The development of the human mind and personality is dependent on the cycles of the Moon. In taking a step further to bring a confluence between the inner and the greater consciousness, it's imperative for us to understand the meaning of what Jupiter and the Moon can signify in each phase. From a traditional point of view, this is a very positive cycle altogether because the Moon's association with a natural benefic is considered auspicious. Therefore, all the phases will certainly have a softer approach towards shaping our inner consciousness to bring it in perfect sync with the greater consciousness.

BRIDGING INNER CONSCIOUSNESS AND GREATER CONSCIOUSNESS

We, as humans, are mostly aware of what we need from a materialistic standpoint and this seems to be the most important learning in today's world of education. Everyone is aware of where to invest and how to make returns. On the other hand, spiritual development and answering the inner call to meet the greater mind within ourselves is often something that lies deep inside the mental apparatus. Whether we ignore it consciously or not is irrelevant, but the fact is we tend to forget the greater learning and the need to bridge the inner consciousness and the greater consciousness for the most part.

The realization of the inner call to meet the greater mind is the point where an individual is ready for actual personality and spiritual development. It's important to have an open and universal mindset while we think about ourselves. The Moon puts our own needs and greeds in the forefront, which we promptly oblige. On the other hand, Jupiter adds the social quotient where someone else is benefitted by what we do. By saying spiritual development, we do not mean sitting in front of a godly figure and meditating. It's all about how to make simple, everyday life easier for someone else while we also make it easier for ourselves. "Take pleasure in one thing and rest in it," said Marcus Aurelius, "in passing from one social act to another social act, thinking of god."[9]

As we write this, COVID-19 is a deadly virus that's been causing havoc around the world. The way China is dealing with this disease is so Jupiterian. Wuhan is the district that initially reported the most cases of the coronavirus. More than 8,000 doctors and about as many nurses and attendees were deployed across China to treat and deal with infected patients. The Jupiterian part here is that the doctors, nurses, and attendees were also vulnerable to the disease by working closely with the patients. However, humanity takes the front seat here as the medical personnel realize the purpose of their birth. The Chinese government pledged to build a hospital (a 269,000-square-foot facility) in 10 days. The entire world was struck hearing it but even more struck when news came out that the Chinese actually did it. They built a huge hospital facility in just 10 days, to isolate and treat the people affected by the coronavirus. The staff who built this huge facility worked tirelessly without adequate sleep or food. The builders slept wherever they worked and did not demand anything, not even that their basic needs be met. What a mammoth contribution to humanity. This is a living example of bridging the Moon and Jupiter. The Moon signifies the people themselves while Jupiter represents higher thinking. The emotional Moon-mind has clearly gotten in touch with the Jupiterian potential.

MOON-JUPITER PHASES

NEW PHASE (0–45 DEGREES APART) AND THE NEW CONJUNCTION

Individuals born during the first phase of the Moon-Jupiter cycle are likely to bridge the inner consciousness and greater consciousness much better than anyone else because it is so natural to them, and they don't need to make a conscious effort to achieve it. This phase instills optimism and gives the feeling of being in the right place at the right time. The confident nature of individuals in this phase can also make them very generous and forthright. Nothing really dampens the spirit during this phase. Moon-Jupiter new phase people are sowing a seed that potentially will have the legs to go a long way in shaping their life at both internal and external levels.

With this being the start of something new and spectacular, the lucky phase involving two soft planets will enable the individual to make connections with some important people who will help them plan and organize their activities and way of life to align with their purpose. Spiritual dosage is just perfect during this period due to the inbuilt quality of compassion and acceptance. This is a very energetic phase where the seeds are sown with supreme confidence that they might grow into something with tremendous influence and potential in the future.

This phase marks the beginning of the integration of personal and spiritual outlook towards life. Kindness and generosity will be a major feature of character attributes of those living through this phase. From the outside perspective, it might seem as if these people make life seem so simple. Jupiter's connection with the emotional mind brings in the much-needed hydration in the heart, which makes Moon-Jupiter new phase people forgiving in nature. With so many things to feel happy about, life is full of zeal at this point in the bridging of inner consciousness and greater consciousness. There is freedom and confidence as they set the path for the future phases of life.

CRESCENT PHASE (45–90 DEGREES APART)

With the Moon a considerable distance away from Jupiter, but still forming a crucial relationship with it, it will carry forward the experience of the previous phase while being influenced by the current phase. This is the most energetic phase in terms of effort put in by the individual to achieve what they set out to accomplish. While this phase brings a lot to feel good about, it also brings a considerable number of situations where some important decisions need to be made. At times, a lack of clarity might creep in due to the exceeding number of alternatives available to choose from. Of course, Jupiter and the Moon are all about the abundance of resources available to the individual. Moon-Jupiter crescent phase people will make connections with the people who can bring about a significant turning point or pivot in life or matters that the person is currently working through. The energetic nature of the individual during this phase enables them to remain open to various changes in initial plans that they might have to accept due to some unavoidable circumstances, but ultimately for good. At times, they may be intimidated by some of the small things that could appear to be a disturbing element or anything that creates resistance. But the confidence of the individual is so high that they likely won't pay much attention to rectify or eliminate the disturbance.

Relationships with friends and relatives are usually very cordial and support is available from all corners. One of the important facets of this phase is the sense of empathy the individual has developed over a period of time. It helps them understand the needs and problems of others who are connected to them on an emotional level. Nothing works out that is not connected to the individual at an emotional level precisely because the Moon is the emotional mind and Jupiter expands the beneficial qualities of the emotional mind. Moon-Jupiter crescent phase people won't shy away from speaking the truth publicly and the preaching of their own spiritual outlook and way of life might be evident. These individuals tend to be talkative and it's hard not to pay attention to them or to contain them within specific limits. Having said that, they're generally strong and intelligent emotionally, provided the Moon is well placed in the natal chart. This is the phase of constant searching for growth and upliftment.

FIRST QUARTER PHASE (90–135 DEGREES APART)

Physically and mentally, this is the most fruitful and enjoyable phase where things just flow easily in various aspects of the individual's life. After keeping on track based upon a plan and making necessary changes, this will be a phase where consolidation of the modified position and further growth takes place. This is also one of those phases where there's a lot of support available to the individual at various stages because of their own kindness and generosity.

During this phase, the individual reaches out to make connections that are beyond their limited circle of people or community. This brings in a great deal of new learning and experience, which eventually works out for the betterment of the individual. Moon-Jupiter first quarter phase people are generally emotionally self-assured. Even though they're definitely classically emotional, we surely will see a strength of emotional intelligence where emotions are well managed and emotional situations are well dealt with. The individual will go out of the way to help someone who is dealing with emotional challenges. Their positive outlook will attract many people from the outside and this will turn out to be a characteristic feature of the individual that can end up being helpful to others on a large scale. The right people show up at just the right time.

Moon-Jupiter first quarter phase people usually remain courteous and are aware of their limitations in every walk of their lives. Even while extending themselves to help others due to their generous nature, they know when to stop offering their hand as they subtly make sure that their care is not considered an interruption.

GIBBOUS PHASE (135–180 DEGREES APART)

The individual climbs higher on the ladder of growth at both inner and greater levels. Moon-Jupiter gibbous phase people don't seem to look back to where they came from as they usually focus on their future path. This can sometimes lead to some hasty steps as they might actually lose sight of vision. People can get carried away during this phase with what they've seen and the knowledge of where they're headed can result in some carelessness. This is the potential downside of this phase, but overall, this is a very fruitful phase in terms of results if the right decisions are made.

In Moon-Jupiter gibbous phase, the individual can turn out to be more receptive and adaptable to situations than they were before. Even though this phase doesn't usually bring as major a change or shift as the crescent phase, a situation could arise where some critical changes might have to be made and the change will result in a shifting of gears in a positive direction. The adjustments made during gibbous phase can further elevate the good conditions of the individual's life. Self-analysis and self-improvement are the driving forces during this phase.

Moon-Jupiter gibbous phase people might also encounter some differences with the greater consciousness as their personal ideologies and understanding of the inner consciousness is modified or more refined. This is very reconcilable, but the individual does generally need to learn to trust their instincts when it comes to dealing with the social side of their life. It's important to ensure it doesn't defeat or interfere with the purpose of their greater goal or consciousness.

FULL PHASE (180–225 DEGREES APART) AND THE OPPOSITION

While the inner consciousness and the greater consciousness are opposite each other during this phase, this is the most matured period where the individual reaps the benefits of all that they've created or accomplished so far. Moon-Jupiter full phase people usually nurture everyone they come across and tend to be a positive figure for others to look up to. Even though the benefits in this phase are many, the energy can be considerably slower than in the earlier phases. But the generosity and benevolent qualities are much more abundant than before.

Now that things are steadier and not needing much monitoring, there may be assumptions that the individual is ready to work for other causes, which might not necessarily be true. Generosity is inbuilt, but at times the individual gets frustrated and doesn't like receiving instructions regarding social matters. This is precisely because the inner and greater consciousness are opposite each other and there's a significant difference between them that often needs reconciliation. Oppositions are always about integrating what seems like opposing forces but are, in fact, one shared continuum of energy. The basic concept of polarity plays out in this phase and individuals are gaining more awareness through anything that appears to be the "other."

Depending upon the condition of the Moon and Jupiter, the mindset oscillates back and forth in terms of dealing with inner personal feelings and feelings that are related to greater causes. The fact is, during this phase, individuals are typically more careful in extending their hand because the Moon is self-aware and more independent again, having traveled as far away from Jupiter as it gets. By the time it reaches the opposition it has a better vantage point. The Moon is driven by experiences, which means the individual's mindset is driven by past experiences. But Jupiter cannot be ignored in the bright light of full phase and the relationship between the inner and greater consciousness can truly begin to blossom.

DISSEMINATING PHASE (225–270 DEGREES APART)

Individuals living through Moon-Jupiter disseminating phase will have their inner consciousness attempt to override the greater consciousness due to the pressure of the Moon. Self-protective mechanisms will come into place, but the individual will be generous enough to share their safety net with others as well. Despite being self-protective, these individuals are happy to look out for others and hear their thoughts because the Moon is caring and wants the best of all. To have the best of all, the individual needs to have various options to choose from. It can't get the best by itself; it has to work with others and within the system. Its best is ultimately tied to the best for all, and the Moon is an active participant in creating these better circumstances.

Emotions can run high in this phase and becoming overly emotional might backfire at times, so it's important to bring them down and approach things from a higher level. The fact that the Moon is now catching up with Jupiter from the other side can manifest as the Moon's reactions and voice being louder and firmer than Jupiter. Physical touch and sharing feelings are important during this phase because they calm and prevent too much rigidity. It's important to let things go at times during this phase for self-betterment. Detachment is not always negative; it does good at times.

Although it might seem otherwise, relationships with others in the community are not so difficult. There's a natural drive to be a meaningful member of society and seek to contribute to a collective vision. It's important for Moon-Jupiter disseminating phase people not to push the agenda too far as others might feel the enlightened self-interest and accuse the individual of being selfish. These accusations can hurt deeply at an emotional level because the individual is naturally quite sensitive to judgment. Reaching a maximum growth point in the cycle, the individual will be much more aware of what is happening around them and things will be under control without much new growth. This is the time to resolve conflicts that arose due to the non-reconcilement of inner and greater consciousness.

LAST QUARTER PHASE (270–315 DEGREES APART)

This is an emotionally driven phase where the sense of generosity and compassion is very high. Maturity of mind is such that the individual feels the need to guide and help everyone who seeks their wisdom. This is not a phase of growth, but this is the phase where reality is understood, and the individual will be ready to trust others as well. Satisfaction is attained easily during this phase and usually, there are no unrealistic expectations of anything. Even though material growth is limited, personal inner growth is very much in the cards and there is no stopping it at all.

Relationships with people and humanity as a whole keep improving and are probably at their best during this phase. Faith is cultivated in the mind toward all those who are closely associated with the individual, and the trust factor is well established. With the amount of compassion and love shown by the individual, people around will be ready to oblige with help at any point in time. There is obvious reciprocity here. Others are responding to the goodwill the individual has extended them in other situations or lifetimes.

Moon-Jupiter last quarter phase is not about dealing with internal matters on their own, it's all about dealing with internal matters that are influenced by external situations. The individual's emotions and personal views will drive their decision making at various junctures in life, but there's a reorientation towards a more integrated inner and greater consciousness. Moreover, they're influenced by past experiences in this phase and generally act based upon what they feel has happened in a similar situation in the past. Taking responsibility for their prior actions and understanding why they made those choices help them aspire to a better future. This phase can be a profound awakening and lays the road to self-actualization.

BALSAMIC PHASE (315–360 DEGREES APART) AND THE BALSAMIC CONJUNCTION

Emotional overdose can overtake the greater consciousness and this phase is a battle where some major efforts are made to reconcile the inner and greater consciousness. When some things are not in line with the initial expectations of the individual, the heart will itch to bring unity between the inner calling and the greater calling. This is a prelude to the next Moon-Jupiter conjunction, which begins a new phase and entirely new cycle.

With the Moon overpowering Jupiter, emotions run high, but the idea of considering the greater call is always present in the subconscious, and individuals will not neglect to heed it. Although physical energy runs low, just like in all balsamic phases, the will to get things set for the coming dawn will not fade away. This is the phase where a lot of thinking and processing goes on and the individual lies low rather than projecting themselves out into the open. It's a closing period where they can best help themselves by turning within, for that's indeed the call of the hour.

A new beginning always first saw an end and every great beginning will someday have to witness an end. Moon-Jupiter balsamic phase people have developed maturity and will have an instinctive feeling that they have to start all over again. They prepare for this both mentally and physically, equipping themselves with necessary resources. In this phase of retreat, the individual gains confidence, courage, optimism, and wisdom to plan for the future.

SEVEN
The Moon and Saturn: Bridging Abundance and Limitations

Saturn, a hard taskmaster, enables us to make crucial life choices at critical junctures in life. We have to live through the pain and suffering to reach the goal of our lives. The Moon's relationship with Saturn takes us through various phases of psychological filtering where we end up coming out as a more complete person through a wide range of constructive and difficult experiences. These experiences define our strength of character and give us the opportunity to be human beings who act with integrity, discipline, compassion, and selflessness.

While we take charge of shaping our destiny, we have to undergo the hardships that Saturn presents in our quest to beat the odds and become what we were born to be. Having confidence in our abilities and trusting others without unreasonable doubt is something that Saturn teaches us, alongside lessons in handling limitations and overcoming pessimism. Seeking the truth is something that we're all doing in this spiritual experience, as our own avatar and human, and we stand equipped to accomplish it as we live through the activated configuration of the Moon and Saturn.

SATURN: INTEGRITY AND MASTERY

Saturn is the most feared planet in astrology. Even a layman understands Saturn as a dreadful planet that's believed to bring misery to humankind. However, there's a much better and encouraging philosophical side to Saturn. On the other hand, we're not trying to maintain an overly positive outlook for everything. We need a healthy dose of realism and practicality. Things can be really tricky at times, and they remain tricky no matter what. Saturn is a cold planet that's far away from the luminaries, which philosophically indicates the condition of being bereft of vision and nourishment.

"Saturn is associated with all that holds us down, or makes us afraid," said Robert Wilkinson in *Saturn: Spiritual Master, Spiritual Friend,* "and those times in life when we must do something we really don't want to do. Saturn doesn't seem to cut us much slack, and when it's active, we often feel stuck, limited, or held back."[10]

Saturn brings in the reality of limitations to almost everything. Limitations are not the hurdles to our learning and growth. They help us realize what's no longer needed or not serving us. In our journey of self-discovery and liberation, we tend to carry too much, shouldering weight that isn't necessary and just keeps us down. Saturn creates a boundary in order to drop all those unwanted burdens from our backs and helps us travel swiftly, lightly, and with wisdom.

CYCLES OF THE MOON AND SATURN

> "Within the field of consciousness, life flows, in other words, changes take place, energy is released in actions and reactions. This "psychic energy" which is contained and operates in the field of consciousness within the boundaries of my ego, set symbolically by Saturn is represented astrologically by the Moon. The Moon is that portion of the Sun which is enclosed by Saturn—if such an astronomically peculiar sentence may be allowed. It is that portion of the life energy of the total being which I am aware of as myself, as the conscious ego which I am. Saturn refers to the abstract structure of this ego. The Moon pours into this "psychic energy" and the result is a conscious entity, a particular living entity. The relation Saturn-Moon is therefore the relation: form-to-energy."
>
> —Dane Rudhyar, *The Astrology of Personality*[11]

"Within" is a word that implies limitations and there are many limitations in our lives in general, irrespective of the outlook we have towards life. *Field of consciousness* is a very important term that directly refers to the amount of energy involved. We cannot vouch for or impose our thoughts on this. You may have a different opinion and gladly disagree. We emphasize our own opinion that time is not greater than consciousness. For us, consciousness is God, or whatever you like to call it. Someone has indeed created time and that someone is God, consciousness. Just as time and space are one, God and Consciousness are one and the same. Our limitation is time, and we operate within that limitation, at least for now. Saturn and the Moon bring together an energy that molds our inner being with time as a result of multiple experiences within the field of consciousness.

The Moon plays a major role in altering the course of the general mentality of human beings. The Moon's position in the chart and its condition reflect the psychological makeup of a person and offer unassailable insights to an astrologer with regards to personality. The Moon rules what we want, and it also determines our attitude towards what we want, which basically brings out a character from inside us that's called personality. Astronomically, the Moon is a reflector of light. Applying that same philosophy will help us understand that the Moon is a major reflector of a person's personality. The Moon reveals the components of a person's psychological makeup.

BRIDGING ABUNDANCE AND LIMITATIONS

Saturn takes about 30 years to pass through all the zodiac signs and the Moon takes about 30 days. This symbolic 30 days/30 years ideology reminds us of the popular astrological technique, secondary progressions. While transiting Saturn's entry into the sign of one's natal Saturn marks the Saturn return, which occurs about every 29.5 years, the secondary progressed Moon also takes about the same amount of time to complete its cycle around the entire zodiac. So while we're embarking upon the journey of our Saturn return, our progressed Moon also returns to its natal position/phase. Saturn sets limitations from one side and the Moon, based upon its position and configuration with other planets, offers us resources to get through the cycle.

This symbolic astronomical relationship offers a treasure hoard of astrological insights that help an astrologer address the nature and quality of life of an individual from a psychological standpoint with a clear purpose. Moon-Saturn cycles deal with the evolution of a person in their human experience. Understanding the purpose of one's life becomes a major theme of this cycle as they're forced to make significant life choices and are bound to the results. This cycle teaches us how to depart from people or things we've held dear for quite some time. We hardly have any options to choose from at any point, while analyzing this cycle, which is basically why it seems to be tough. As humans, we develop attachments to many things and many people, especially those who are familiar and comfortable to us. At times, reality hits hard when we need to take a different path—one that requires leaving behind some of what's not needed in order to enter the next stage of our lives. We don't usually know or consciously recognize this, and it can feel like pressure, trigger fear, and manifest as depression. There's no question the Moon-Saturn cycle can stabilize, mature, and teach us through some tough knocks to the ego. The illusion is that what appears to be in abundance might not last long and what appears to be a limitation might turn out to be a strength as we're forced to work with and adjust to restrictions during various stages of the Moon-Saturn cycle. We might have to make choices in life that require a great deal of commitment and accountability because Saturn indicates responsibility.

MOON-SATURN PHASES

NEW PHASE (0–45 DEGREES APART) AND THE NEW CONJUNCTION

The Moon and Saturn in new phase conjunction is a very critical beginning where the force of Saturn hits metaphorical Moon in the face with a stream of reality checks. What once appeared to be simple and normal would appear to be an issue today. What appeared abundant will now seem scarce. Emotions that were easy to handle some time ago will suddenly appear to be hard to manage. The odds will creep up from all four corners. Fatigue will rise and pose questions about the physical condition and resilience required to "fight out" this tricky phase.

Due to such crunches from all corners, individuals in the Moon-Saturn new phase will usually take a defensive position in most life scenarios. They're easily hurt during this phase and if they come to know that someone doesn't trust their abilities, they might take it straight to the heart. In such instances, they can be incredibly sensitive. In this phase, the risk is in being too fragile, especially if they face trouble with other people in terms of faith and trustworthiness.

However, all of these sensitivities and fragilities are merely reactions to the psychological beliefs that things are troublesome because they're used to more comfort and ease. The reality of not having the same comforts and ease in life is hard to accept, especially from a psychological standpoint. Mental fatigue is more of a factor and causes more problems than physical fatigue. So it's important for Moon-Saturn new phase people to endure the perceived pain and create a win for themselves by sticking in there and learning to see things and what's really good for them in a new way.

CRESCENT PHASE (45–90 DEGREES APART)

This phase is generally easier and less hectic than the Moon-Saturn new phase since things have already settled down a bit. Rather than complaining about limitations and scarce resources, crescent phase individuals will be inclined to go ahead and search for what they need. Such pursuits keep them occupied and therefore less susceptible to emotional battles despite the fact that they can get really emotional in any given situation.

Individuals often turn out to be more organized and controlled during the Moon-Saturn crescent phase. They will have a thing or two to prove to the external world, especially if they were taken for granted in the past, and these external motivations will keep them going. Since emotions run high, they care a great deal for those around them but don't necessarily express it, which is a perfectly Saturnian way of manifesting things. However, honesty is paramount when it comes to any kind of relationship, and they do not take it for granted.

Even though they're emotional, these individuals will be capable of making tough decisions at crucial junctures in life. However, there won't be much showing off in their actions and expressions. They have a tendency to lie low and accomplish what they set out to do, which is an admirable quality to possess. Discipline and a structured way of living is the key to moving through this phase, and Saturn will push the Moon (inner being) to remain that way.

FIRST QUARTER PHASE (90–135 DEGREES APART)

In this crucial phase, individuals can be forced to make changes they feel they weren't ready for, especially at an emotional level. One of the most important things to remember is that even though they may be pushed to the edge from all sides, there are some people who support them in doing what they can to master the situation. However, this might be a case when they need to move away from the people who've been strong pillars of emotional support. This could be a major pivot point, as they prepare to make a big turn from their regular course of life. This is a phase where individuals may be forced out of their comfort zones.

In due course, Moon-Saturn first quarter phase people won't be necessarily happy in making the shift as it might appear to have been forced upon them. Frustration will run high and confidence will be significantly lower than it was in the crescent phase. The downside is, they might end up venting frustration at the people around them and develop a judgmental attitude towards life and people in general. It's important to keep irritation and the temper in check at all times, especially when the chips are down.

Yet things will move forward and the individual might use all that creative force to continue doing what they set out to do. And that's the purpose of periods that have a Saturnian focus. To not just think about what we could or should do, but to actually do it. We're called to follow our path with righteousness (dharma) to continue our karma (actions). This path, through its shifts and challenges, is meant to be that way, and this is the road that leads to where we're destined to be.

GIBBOUS PHASE (135–180 DEGREES APART)

While suffering on some level is a common theme when the Moon is influenced by or configured with Saturn, the Moon-Saturn gibbous phase offers a platform to grow in strength as the individual has already learned lessons in detachment and now knows the value of compassion. Handling pain will likely not be as difficult for these people, as they've come a long way and will be equipped to accept reality as it comes, from a psychological standpoint.

Individuals in this phase will be more composed and satisfied when they're extremely focused and also determined to accomplish their tasks. Apart from their regular routine and actions, they're also very well aware of the domestic responsibilities they need to fulfill in the context of their family or those who depend on them. Saturn teaches through experiences and so these individuals can naturally be quite conservative and realistic in their approach. This attitude is largely due to the pitfalls they've faced in life. They know better than to let unanchored optimism blind them to what's actually happening.

As they would have already accepted many changes in life and life direction, Moon-Saturn gibbous phase people might view any upcoming changes as unfavorable and quickly oppose them. This resistance to change is not because they cannot change, it's because of the confidence they have in their current path. It doesn't mean they don't want to face the new things the world wants to show them, but these individuals have already undergone changes and they're dedicated to solidifying, strengthening, and improving upon what they've already established.

FULL PHASE (180–225 DEGREES APART) AND THE OPPOSITION

While the Moon and Saturn are in opposition to each other, things that appeared to be in order can seem to start falling apart. Doubt arises in the minds of these individuals regarding whether they're capable enough to handle such situations. Mental conservatism can slowly turn into limitation and fear. Decision making becomes really challenging during this phase when things seem at odds with each other and there's doubt and confusion. On the positive side, there's a greater awareness and relatability in full phase that opens the door to new levels of cooperation and collaboration in relationships. The integration of the Moon and Saturn can create a safe and productive environment for life and love to thrive.

Apart from the tendency to be rigid and reluctant to accept what comes their way, these individuals are also influenced by possible negative results of their past actions. Anything in full phase is subject to the full shining spotlight, illuminating what's been kept in the dark. As experience influences the decisions of these people, they have to be careful not to over-rely on their own experiences and refuse to learn from others. They might not trust anyone else to help them make the best choices or decisions. They can feel that not many people could actually help them in such scenarios. Most of these feelings are just assumptions and Moon-Saturn full phase people can support themselves by getting other opinions and asking for help when they can't do something on their own.

Sometimes, individuals in this phase don't have a fallback plan or plan B. They just stick to one particular route and if that fails, they go into a shell and doubt their abilities. Just a little bit of tweaking here and there to accept something different and having another alternative plan will help them in the long run. This is also a classic Saturnian manifestation as they're not always abundant in terms of ideas and can be limited by their own mindset in facing limitations. In this state of culmination, it's important to have a healthy balance of abundance and limitations in order to respond to life with more ease and grace. And limiting of oneself based on assumptions is something to release in this phase.

DISSEMINATING PHASE (225–270 DEGREES APART)

Moon-Saturn disseminating phase is a period of retrospection and realization that we can't always use the same approach in life. We need flexibility and to learn to adapt to and work within the structures set around us. We have to be the ones who move. The attitude of these individuals is reasonably optimistic as a lot has happened over a period of time and the course is already set in motion, which really cannot be undone at this point. This is one phase where individuals are more open to other ideas and will also have a relatively positive way of dealing with people in terms of trusting and working with them.

The biggest limitation prior to the disseminating phase would have been trusting others around them. The fact is we cannot do everything by ourselves and we need various people to travel with us on this journey of life. While we request help on some occasions, we also need to be open to returning the favor when someone needs our help. Moon-Saturn disseminating people understand this reality and life becomes easier as the ability to adapt is much greater.

Resources are relatively easy to acquire and there generally won't be many limitations in what individuals can manifest for themselves during this phase. Authority and responsibility increase on the professional front, which is indicated as Saturn is the natural significator of livelihood and profession. The Moon in configuration with Saturn, especially the trine aspect, gives a comfortable feeling and natural flow regarding work. Decision making is still cautious but much easier than in the opposition because the individual is more open to the ideas of others. They're also naturally drawn to share their wisdom and act with authority.

LAST QUARTER PHASE (270–315 DEGREES APART)

This is a phase where emotions can run very high and seem to rule every part of the individual's life. There's an internal challenge to be objective and see themselves in a more real and true context. Moon-Saturn last quarter phase people identify with their high emotions and these emotions have a considerable impact on those around them. This is yet another phase where individuals may find it difficult to get out of their comfort zone. Unlike the gibbous phase, they won't have a choice to stay where they are in terms of leading life. They're on the precipice of a breakthrough in awareness and anytime we unconsciously sense such a shift, the ego responds with resistance. The very form these individuals take and how they embody their ideals and energy may not fit anymore. There can be an inner questioning: "If I'm not that, then who am I?"

This phase will demand difficult decision making in terms of choosing the path they're going to travel for some time. This comes as a tough reality check to the individual as they may be completely unaware of what is happening around them during the greater part of life. Saturn teaches the importance of being aware through strenuous and burdensome trials and tests and one such test is being open to change. Acceptance is not so common in human beings unless they're spiritually well-inclined. Humans crave more and it's not easy to find a satisfied or contented person. The emotions of Moon-Saturn last quarter phase people will make it hard for them to understand the reality of the situation. They try to stick to their comfort zone, which is a battle that nature will eventually win.

On the other hand, exercising free will during this phase is to remain open to changes no matter how hard it may seem. Enduring pain and suffering, and the associated crisis of awakening, will eventually take these individuals out of their temporary uncomfortable zone into another new comfort zone, within which life makes a significant move. Saturn is a timekeeper and it will not deny, just delay, whatever is destined to be the fruits of the individual. People in this phase have the ability to be radically honest with themselves and come up with creative solutions that make life better not just for themselves, but for the whole planet.

BALSAMIC PHASE (315–360 DEGREES APART) AND THE BALSAMIC CONJUNCTION

In the Moon-Saturn balsamic phase, oppression can take over as Saturn usually forces the individual to face surprising or shocking things. The Moon helps us to visualize only what we want to see in its unchangeable selfish side. Saturn, however, doesn't agree with this ideology and forces the issue with the Moon. What individuals in this phase assumed about life and themselves can disturb their sleep and rise up as fear of failure. This phase is one where the individual understands and realizes that assumptions and presumptions in life can be dangerous. At some stages, life is driven by our mistakes for which we end up paying a dear price. Every action has an equal and opposite reaction.

Individuals in this phase have to deal with the emotional trouble of letting go of whatever burdens they're carrying. The heart doesn't accept burdens at first, but as we pass through this dark tunnel, time teaches us to accept the realities of life. Saturn, with time, helps us deal with many things. Awareness is the biggest lesson of this phase. The number of issues and shocks that individuals need to manage at times like these can be consuming, plaguing them with fatigue and leaving emotional and psychological battle scars. They can develop limited vision, and the tasks they plan or would like to accomplish eventually pile up. There are interruptions from external surroundings and obligations to others that can't be ignored without losing sight of personal deadlines. Reputation on some level may be threatened or even destroyed at this time, dealing another psychological blow to the ego before the individual can begin to rebuild it again.

It's almost as if Saturn is forcing the Moon to face the results of past actions. The Moon is about our mindset and how we feel about our history, and it responds in a nearly pessimistic way. Towards the end of this phase, some individuals may almost, or completely, cross the line of pessimism and reach negativism as a result of the Moon's proximity to Saturn. It all depends on how the Moon chooses to receive Saturn. By accepting defeat at nature's hands, we can maintain sanity because we're not actually losing at anyone's hands, only at the hands of nature or God or consciousness. What we "lost" was just an illusion of something we thought was real. We don't gain anything from sugarcoating, compromising, or consoling ourselves after suffering a defeat or failure from life's uncertainties. This is just a part of what we need to accept in ourselves.

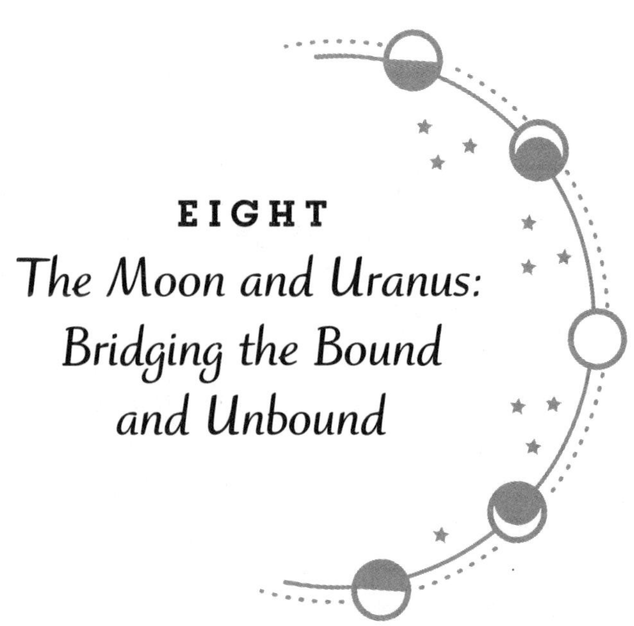

EIGHT
The Moon and Uranus: Bridging the Bound and Unbound

To begin to know what we really are, we must discover what we aren't. The Moon-Uranus cycle is one way to observe the progression of awakening to who we are—to our personal essence that's not defined by anything that happened in the past. The way most of us look at life and ourselves is through history. Our brains are always digging into a giant file cabinet of old thoughts and memories and emotionally reacting to them. We aren't seeing anything as it is now.

Uranus is the unalterable you that remains when all your conditioning is stripped away. It's the you that just IS. Just like clothes and blankets keep your body warm and protected, the Moon is your emotional buffer. It's the part of you that attempts to throw a cloak of protection against anything that threatens your story.

Exploring your Moon-Uranus phase offers insight into how the you that you know and the very real yet unknowable you are working together. One doesn't need to be better. When we judge the ego, we just feed that monster and reinforce our bonds to it. When we become proud of our advanced state of evolution, we've totally missed the point. We're all somewhere in a cycle and phase of individuation. While each of us is unique, we're not that different. And we're all waking up.

THE KNOWN AND UNKNOWN

As we get to planets farther away from the Sun, we enter different territory. Sometimes, astrologers refer to the planets inside Jupiter as personal planets, Jupiter and Saturn as interpersonal, and those outside Saturn as transpersonal. Astrologer Steven Forrest, in his wise words, reminds us that it's all personal—all the planets and how they represent or reflect us are personal.[12] Uranus is personal, just like the Moon. It's best not to get too stuck on words, even when reading them, and especially when working with Uranus. The Uranus in each of us may not be personal in the way the Moon is, but it *definitely* takes its agenda personally. What we're trying to say here is that everything in your birth chart is part of your personal signature, potential, and growth. The outer planets have everything to do with our personal experience of energy fields and consciousness that includes much more than ourselves.

In the introduction to his book, *Uranus—Freedom from the Known*, Jeffrey Wolf Green writes: "The Uranian liberation of our times, collectively speaking, will involve the enlightened awareness that reflects the principle of unity in diversity, not the unity in sameness."[13] The Moon is intimately linked with our past, who we know ourselves to be, and finds comfort in how we're the same as others. In some ways, the history-bound Moon is opposite to Uranus with its drive to liberate from the past, be original and authentic, and celebrate being different. The Moon in evolutionary astrology is a symbol of the ego and Uranus is the drive to decondition. Put them together and we're looking at deconditioning the ego. The phases of these two planets reveal, in part, the stages we're in when it comes to unbinding our egos. As we've already mentioned, the ego isn't something negative that needs to die, but if we choose to look through its eyes and go its way, it will trap us in the past. If we stay rooted in our history and what we think we know ourselves and life to be, there isn't room for real change. Uranus draws us into the realm of the unknown where there's a greater version of ourselves waiting to be discovered and actualized.

URANUS: LOOKING FORWARD NOT BEHIND

Uranus is the planet of individuation and awakening. It awakens in each of us the rebel who's tired of doing things by someone else's rules or conditions. Uranus is your greater mind that's part of and has access to the collective mind. It's the part of you aware that you are consciousness and it takes direction from itself. We sometimes call Uranus the higher mind because it operates in a state of freedom and can witness the other parts of you as they're happening, including your monkey brain. It's objective intelligence, not attached to maintaining anything you've constructed physically, mentally, or emotionally. Nothing can stop it, limit it, or define it. To work with it effectively, you must learn to detach from most of what you've come to believe is true, especially about yourself. The "you" that you've identified with begins to fade away as you observe yourself. You experience the You behind the you.

If you've heard that Saturn represents the boundaries of what we can see, or our visible reality, think again. Under the right conditions, Uranus can be seen with the naked eye. As we learn new things about our solar system, it only seems fitting that we take a new look at the meaning we've assigned to it. This would be the Uranian way; continually shaking ourselves up enough to see how the pieces settle in the present. They might be the same, but just mentally releasing our position on something usually sharpens and broadens our understanding as it comes back together more naturally.

Most things about Uranus are unusual, astronomically and astrologically speaking. It was discovered in 1781 and eventually named after Ouranos, the Greek god of the heavens or sky. Uranus is the only planet named after a Greek god; the rest are named after Roman deities. It's also the only planet that rolls on its side through space. It's so tilted on its axis that it has extreme, long seasons, some lasting twenty years. Uranus also orbits the Sun in the opposite direction of Earth and most other planets. Simply put, it's an archetype that goes its own way.

Uranus in each of us inspires our metamorphoses and knows how we can personally and individually fly. Its role is to shatter anything that's become too crystallized, and in fact, the planet Uranus is an ice giant, made mostly of flowing icy materials. Uranian energy can be abrupt, unpredictable, and not concerned with how it comes across. It's not about pleasing anyone but itself in the course of breaking free and being what it is without censor or restriction. The Uranian impulse and process of individuation do serve humanity, but at its core, it's about the highest expression of self. It's a perfect example of personal work and awakening automatically contributing to the healing and evolution of the planet. The Uranian mind is forward-thinking, unbound by preconceived ideas, and open to radical insights that once received make it impossible to ever go back. As Einstein is quoted as saying, "No problem can be solved from the same level of consciousness that created it." He knew how to use this thing we call Uranus and is, of course, considered a genius.

CYCLES OF THE MOON AND URANUS

The Moon's synodic cycle, or soli-lunar cycle, takes about 29.5 days. Uranus takes 84 years to orbit the Sun. The Moon moves from one sign to another every 2.25 to 2.5 days. Uranus spends about 7 years in each sign. Unless it's at its 7-year transition point, Uranus holds a steady position in the same sign while the Moon goes through many of its complete monthly cycles. The Moon will repeatedly meet Uranus on the same ground over and over again and each time, there's the opportunity for liberation on the most personal, emotional level. Slower-moving planets have time on their side, meaning they have a longer, sustained influence on our evolution. The Moon is focused on the hourly, daily, and monthly external and internal motions. Uranus is aimed at the pivotal phases of our lives, in particular the rites of passage around ages twenty-one, forty-two, sixty-three, and eighty-four. These two bodies in our solar system operate on different timetables and different levels of consciousness. Their interactions with each other reveal the integration and synergy of our human-bound selves and unbound spirit selves. Growth is dependent upon them both.

BRIDGING THE BOUND AND UNBOUND

The Moon is receptive, receiving other energy and then responding to it. It's the heart of our experience. So to receive the unknown of Uranus and become a little more unbound, we have to be kind with ourselves. Our Moon needs don't just disappear because we're awakening to our inner wisdom and authenticity. And working *with* our Moon is the point anyway. Liberation is different for each person and it's important not to invoke a "should" upon others in the name of freedom or growth. What you need and will help you break out of your cage may not do it for someone else. Bridging the bound and unbound isn't a weekend workshop, it's a journey over lifetimes. What do you need in order to take a risk and let go of a false sense of self? A Moon in Cancer might need emotional stability first. Moon in Sagittarius might need to have fun and the promise of adventure. The point is to take care of your Moon-self so there's less fear and resistance in stepping off the metaphorical curb or cliff. The ego doesn't like to be challenged or threatened, which is exactly what happens when the Moon meets Uranus.

While most of us complain about it, we take orders from someone else. It could be at work, from our parents, our partners, the church, or the government—and those are just some common examples. We all exist in a collective system and must learn how to work within it to pursue our personal paths. Each of us, too, must determine how we can become unbound while bound and become free exactly where we are. We each choose our path to freedom and what we must unchain to move in that direction.

Let's take that Sagittarius Moon person who needs to have fun and adventure. If they were shown a path of liberation that involved regimented spiritual book lessons on a regular schedule, do you think they'd want to be free? Freedom is not a destination, it's a way of living and state of mind. It's not determined by your circumstances, although changing some things could be very supportive for you. The Moon can be a good measure of where you get stuck. While it represents what nurtures and feeds you, we always must include the polarity, which can be how you neglect, hinder, or starve yourself. It can also be where and how you wallow around, especially emotionally, and refuse to grow up. Uranus wants more for you and shows your potential and intention to free yourself, first and foremost from yourself.

MOON-URANUS PHASES

NEW PHASE (0–45 DEGREES APART) AND THE NEW CONJUNCTION

Welcome to a new evolutionary cycle of ego liberation. Individuals born in this phase may not be consciously aware their innermost self is entering a major renovation, but they will feel it. As with all new phase signatures, there's little to no external light for guidance. The cycle that's beginning is still a spark of intention and there's no telling how it will progress and ultimately mature and complete. These are the first Uranian knocks that shake the ego foundation represented by the Moon. The Moon and Uranus haven't developed a working relationship yet—it's more like the Moon woke up with Uranus filling its house and now there's no getting away from it. This is especially applicable to the new conjunction, which can manifest like a conglomeration of the two planets, because by degree they're on top of each other. As the Moon starts to move away from Uranus, a sliver of perspective appears, but new phase is primarily instinctual and spontaneous, motivated internally and quite subjective.

Moon-Uranus new phase people can support themselves by exploring their emotions with courage. Their feelings and gut reactions will show them where they have resistance and they need to experience this resistance fully in order to move through it. They're challenging themselves to live a new life, but they have no idea what this means yet. There is never any way other than charging forward with new phase. The influence of Uranus can feel unsettling in the body, sometimes making the individual more jumpy, fidgety, or anxious. With new phase, Uranus is close to the Moon, which is very connected with the physical and emotional bodies. It's also a newer presence and we tend to feel shifting energy most strongly, like when a transiting planet moves into a new house. Uranus is initiating awakening in the most tender and private spaces. The Moon is a fierce protector, hypersensitive to outside threats. Even though Uranus isn't outside the individual, it can feel that way. There might be some chaos, especially psychologically, but it's serving a greater purpose. What the new moon phase person thought was order had become suffocating to the spirit. They've summoned the aspect of themselves ready to turn the ship around, maybe even burn it down if necessary—whatever it takes to "be free to be me."

CRESCENT PHASE (45–90 DEGREES APART)

Crescent is the phase of expansion and early growth that takes serious determination and effort. The greater self is putting pressure on the smaller self to let old habits, ideas, and rules go, but it's so easy to collapse under the pressure and fear. The new phase of initiation is over and now the individual has to start laying the bricks of the new foundation. This is pretty easy to understand when it comes to building a house, but not so clear when it comes to a new level of mental awakening, authenticity, or ego liberation. This is the unconscious challenge the Moon-Uranus crescent phase person faces. It can be helpful to remember that anything that feels comfortable now was once new and threatening. And whatever is pushing the old limits now will one day be ancient itself. Just like many Taurean-flavored situations, crescent phase can demand struggle and the intensity of the struggle is in proportion to how stuck and stubborn the person may be. They're meeting themselves on new ground and the very resistance they hold against the change creates the tension that helps break them out of their confinement.

It might seem like little progress is being made during this phase, but if seen from a greater perspective, there is often a tremendous progression as the individual charges through obstacles. Moon-Uranus crescent phase people are getting intimate with how tightly wound they've become and how they've limited their ability to grow by staying safe and simple. Now, the unbound self is very intent on shifting the whole person a little closer to embodying their true self. The Moon-self with its conditioned self-identity has stood the test of time and will naturally reject and defend against anything it doesn't know it can survive. In addition, the ego-driven self doesn't want to value or recognize what is greater than itself. So, of course, the Uranian impulse to sever the past and challenge anything that's gotten cozy or common is like starting a personal civil war between the conservative and radical parts of the psyche. People in this phase have glimpses of their future selves and can feel their energetic shape and orientation changing, but it's still relatively new. They can help themselves by nurturing any ideas, thoughts, feelings, or experiences that reveal something new about who they are and by creating more freedom to discover themselves without the old roles and labels. Moon-Uranus crescent phase can manifest as the need to produce results that prove all that hard work is paying off—if it were a business, we'd be looking for the money. The value of self-liberation and going one's own way isn't so easy to measure in the material world and may even lead to a loss by traditional standards. But the growth and potential that follows is immeasurable and not left behind when this life ends.

FIRST QUARTER PHASE (90–135 DEGREES APART)

The first quarter phase is the time to test things out and with Moon-Uranus this could be acting out a more liberated self in the world. It's impossible to know what will truly set one free until they try for themselves. It's quite possible that individuals in this phase will blaze forward with conviction about something and then realize it isn't who they are at all. The ego is tricky, and we use it to play games on ourselves all the time. In this phase, the only way to test authenticity is through vulnerability. Moon-Uranus first quarter phase people need to share their uniqueness open-heartedly. When they do, they'll know right away whether it was authentic. If it wasn't, it will fall flat and the individual will know it, even if the audience claps. There may also be times when the person is being true to themselves and letting it show and others don't approve or praise. It's important not to lose heart if things don't go as planned. Part of liberating the conditioned self is recognizing when that conditioning is at play. Gaining that knowledge is worth taking the risk and putting on the show, no matter how it goes.

Self-expression is a theme of the first quarter phase and individuals can feel challenged to put their mark on the world. The caution here is in failing to think first and forcing things. Spontaneous, vulnerable, heart-felt action is absolutely called for, but overdramatizing and demanding attention is not. Those in Moon-Uranus first quarter phase are trying to validate their own self-liberated selves. They want to see what their more authentic self looks like and how it behaves. This is a very subjective phase in the sense that it's all about how the external environment responds to what the individual does and is. It's important for them to own the results of their experiments and recognize they're working out *their own* issues. There's a wonderful opportunity here for the ego to show itself more clearly and honestly as it rises to the challenges posed by Uranus and its intolerance for the façade. It can be the real start of the two working together.

GIBBOUS PHASE (135–180 DEGREES APART)

The bridging of the known and unknown that began in the new phase is now approaching its culmination. The current relationship between the bound and unbound parts of the self has been integrating for some time now. If we stick with the Moon being the part of us that receives and reacts to everything and Uranus as our greater consciousness or higher mind, the integration of the two is the human capacity to receive and reflect greater consciousness. No wonder we see the Moon as mysterious. It's where it all happens as the past and future converge in the present. Is there anything the Moon can't hold? Those in Moon-Uranus gibbous phase are feeling all the ways the past and future, known and unknown, bound and unbound don't fit together. Anything that didn't go well in the previous first quarter phase is under careful review. As we've mentioned, this phase is infused with Virgoan energy and Moon-Uranus gibbous phase people are trying to understand this newly self-liberated or awakened state they find themselves in, and to deal with all the ways they think it can be better.

Imagine you were told you'd be living in the current state of your personal awakening, self-liberation, and authenticity for the next five lifetimes. This is made up of course, but it gets close to what it can feel like in the Moon-Uranus gibbous phase. People in this phase don't want to go forward without doing everything they can to get it right. It's common to feel inadequate and unprepared for what's to come, which makes perfect sense considering the nature of the unknown. While it's necessary to go through this time of self-questioning, editing, and critiquing, it's also healthy to let go of unrealistic standards and expectations. First of all, standards and expectations are contrary to the Uranian impulse and second, it will just suck up all the energy that is better spent clearing out limiting beliefs and attachments. Even small adjustments during this phase have the power to change everything, especially adjustments in perspective. Moon-Uranus gibbous phase people are on the precipice of a new life because they'll be looking at it with new awareness. Whatever they can do now to clear their vision and see more of their truth will be a gift not just to themselves, but to all the lives they're about to touch.

FULL PHASE (180–225 DEGREES APART) AND THE OPPOSITION

The ego has reached a peak of liberation. The Moon and Uranus have reached their farthest distance apart, giving them an unobstructed, full view of each other. Just like a full moon, the full phase represents the light of consciousness and in this case, is shining on consciousness itself. Moon-Uranus full phase people are learning to see their innermost selves more objectively. The point is not to rationalize the irrational, although they might try. Their liberation comes through awareness. This phase of awakening will reveal more clearly where they've reached a summit or plateau in deconditioning their ego and integrating their higher mind. The preceding four phases, or the waxing half of the cycle, was a very active time in re-shaping the ego orientation. Whether individuals recognize it, they've just been through an ego rebirth and all the growing pains that follow. This doesn't have to look like a radical reorientation to everything, but on some level, there's been a shift. As we grow, we're with ourselves every moment, so change rarely seems dramatic. It's like putting on 30 pounds. When someone sees you for the first time since you put on the weight, they can't help but notice. But for you, it accumulated over time and you've been adjusting to it along the way. Now, imagine you used to try and prove you were right about everything. You recognized it wasn't a healthy habit for you, and by whatever means you chose, you've let that pattern go. By the time you fully appreciate how you've let that go, the hard work in getting there is over, but the benefits or results are just beginning to show. This is the nature of full phase.

With words like *culmination* and *fulfillment*, we'd expect to see a more liberated, authentic version of self in the Moon-Uranus full phase, but there's no guarantee that the Uranian impulse to liberate was effective in breaking free of ego conditioning. We know the individual made an attempt to rattle their own cage, but that energy can also manifest as rebelling against the rebel. What we know is that however the Moon and Uranus functions are complementing or opposing each other, they've hit a limit of growth. The remainder of the cycle is about learning, sharing, applying, accepting, and finally, releasing. Individuals in full phase are learning about their own state of mental freedom through the mirror of others. As always, projection is likely, particularly if they have not unbound themselves, ignoring the inner prompting of the soul. This makes it easy to blame others for holding them back or limiting their freedom. Becoming aware of how we haven't moved beyond old conditioning and continue to insulate ourselves from beneficial change is sobering. It's also honest. Moon-Uranus full phase people have a natural gift for helping others work with their dueling motivations to stay safe in what they know and unleash from anything that binds them to the past. They can support themselves by paying attention to what they see in others and how others respond to them. The external world reflects their inner world. And they're doing the same for others. This is the time to gain a greater understanding of what seems at odds by seeing how it's actually working together.

DISSEMINATING PHASE (225–270 DEGREES APART)

Disseminating phase is generally about sharing wisdom and working within whatever structures are in place. It requires learning to play by someone else's rules and discovering how they aren't such a good fit. Since we're talking about Moon-Uranus, one's state of ego liberation and awakening, this phase is motivated by the call to use it in service of the community. All the wisdom that's been gained from this entire cycle is not just for personal freedom. Our individual growth determines what we have to contribute to others and affects the collective. That's why every little shift in awareness toward more truth is so powerful. Those in Moon-Uranus disseminating phase are learning where and how their personal state of consciousness can best benefit society. This always requires working within structure because society is built upon structures. The individual is faced with navigating collective physical, organizational, and mental structures. And, of course, they also face the personal structures of every person in whichever group they're serving.

By this point in the cycle, the Moon is headed back toward Uranus; the return trip is underway. There's still some distance to go, but the sense of return brings a natural accounting of how the journey was successful and what there is to show for it. How the results of personally awakening to greater consciousness are benefitting the world is now in question. The Moon-Uranus disseminating phase person is not always working in a career or organization. There are many ways to work within structures. Families have them, relationships have them, and everywhere we go, they're there. The key to this phase is the "working within" them. It emphasizes that evolution in this phase comes through applying the state of self-liberation to the norms versus bucking at the system or avoiding it altogether. This takes determination, patience, and ability to see the bigger picture. And, when putting oneself in these situations, there's a risk of letting ambition, material desires, and a craving for respect suppress the self-liberation and awakened state. When this happens, the person can become depressed, because deep down they know they've sacrificed their authenticity. They can also become aware of the ways they've become rigid in the name of freedom and change.

Individuals in Moon-Uranus disseminating phase can support themselves by taking ownership of their ego evolution. This includes the entire process with its liberation and conditioning, including new conditioning that is always part of the equation. They can lead by example, drawing upon age and experience (from this lifetime and others) to be guides and mentors for others. An elder is a beautiful embodiment of this phase. We don't mean an elder as someone who is simply old, but someone who younger or less experienced people want to learn from. And a wise elder does not mean someone who's transcended their ego. Quite the opposite; it's someone who's learned to integrate it with maturity.

LAST QUARTER PHASE (270–315 DEGREES APART)

The last quarter phase with its Aquarian flavor is a phase of liberation, which makes it a liberator of our so-called liberation. You might be wondering what we do with that, but it's much less complicated than it sounds. Basically, the awakened consciousness is subject to more consciousness. This is exciting because it creates the perfect recipe for breakthroughs in awareness. We talked about the potential of becoming rigid through liberation in the previous phase. It's a real obstacle, just spend time with any Aquarius. The impulse to untether from the past in search of a new future eventually ends up creating a new present, which quickly becomes the past. Since we're nearing the completion of this entire Moon-Uranus cycle, we're definitely looking in the rearview mirror, at least in part. Moon-Aquarius last quarter phase people are challenged to see themselves through a crystal lens that can amplify and magnify the truth. This lens can examine each facet of the psyche in macro vision. This is not a Virgoan analysis or Scorpionic laser focus. It's a greater perspective that helps the individual see, almost impersonally, how much more potential they have to be free.

Re-orientation is a word we've used for the last quarter phase and it encompasses the heart of its essence. Through the waning half of the cycle, the contents we're working with haven't changed, but how we've used them, what we make of them, and our perception of them has been under constant review. Re-orientation won't technically change the contents either, but you could fool anyone that it has, including yourself, because a shift in perception is a shift in reality. The contents in the Moon-Uranus cycle are the emotional body with its body-mind influences and the higher mind; bound and unbound aspects of self. These aren't changing, consciousness doesn't change, so what *is* changing about us? We know change is constant. But what part of us is doing the changing? This is the type of contemplation that arises in the last quarter phase and the questions, not the answers, blow the creative doors open. Freedom from freedom sounds silly, but to someone in this phase, it will likely make sense. We mean freedom from the conditioned definition of freedom. Just the idea that we're seeking freedom implies on some level that we're not free. There can be an existential crisis in this phase because the ceiling and floor disappear on what we thought we were and knew. We have to reconsider what truly has meaning and purpose. The individuals in this phase have to rediscover that for themselves and then do their best to embody it for the greater good of all humankind.

BALSAMIC PHASE (315–360 DEGREES APART) AND THE BALSAMIC CONJUNCTION

There's an ending in every beginning and a beginning in every ending. Energetically, nothing ends; we know it transforms. And here we reach the end of the Moon-Uranus cycle, where our precious self-liberation and awakening recede into the blur. This whole cycle of ego deconditioning and bridging the known with the unknown is attached to a self. Anything interacting with the Moon is ultra-personal and hits close to home. How we receive and react to those things is reflected in our moods and behaviors. During the balsamic phase, there's a natural release of self-importance. The ego has been under the same period of reconstruction long enough that the person can more easily let go of attachments. This doesn't mean old patterns and habits completely dissolve, but less identification with the ego means less necessity for its vices. Even if the new intention for awakened living and liberation from the past was never actualized, there is nothing wrong. Life will go on. It's possible for Moon-Uranus balsamic phase people to experience an unconditional acceptance of the past and almost psychic sense about the future. As with any dying or transition phase, we still have some power to consider what we leave behind and what we take with us.

How we leave something is how we begin the next thing. Dropping old emotional baggage, forgiving self and others, and making peace with history helps clear the way for more enlightened passage, but there's something more. The more authentic, truthful, and real we are with ourselves, the more we burn through old karma. Radical honesty and living our truth are clean; they don't leave anything to resolve later.

Moon-Uranus balsamic phase people have the opportunity to reach a new level of alignment within themselves, lessening the distance between their egos and greater awareness or consciousness. When the illusion of separation is unveiled, conditioning and deconditioning don't even exist. Most of us aren't living in this space yet, but if you can imagine it, you're closer than you think. It might sound like individuals in this phase are here to bypass humanity, but not even close. They're here to accept and embrace it so intimately that there's no room for tension. Balsamic phase always points the compass inward to hear and feel the wisdom of the soul. Awakening sounds like discovering something new, but from the balsamic phase view, it's what's left when each layer of the unreal and inauthentic is stripped away. If you're wondering if the ego actually needs liberation, you're feeling the potential of this phase. We're all returning to what is.

NINE
The Moon and Neptune: Bridging Time and Timelessness

The one and All are the same, but it would be impossible to know that if we had no separate experiences of ourselves. The Moon-Neptune cycle is just one way of looking at how our perceptions of these different aspects of ourselves interact. The bridging of the one and All is happening in our minds, just like everything else we "see" in the universe. The only reason we need a bridge is for our minds. This doesn't change anything we go through or how real it feels. But when you work with Moon-Neptune, something deep inside you doesn't even hear the words; they don't matter. With all the differences we'll look at, the Moon and Neptune still have some powerful things in common. They don't need or even buy into logic. They speak the language of the heart and soul. And they know the way home.

Now we're getting even more out there in the solar system—farther than the naked human eye can see. Neptune is the most distant planet from the Sun that we've discovered. It's linked with mysticism, spirituality, and inspiration. The mysterious, whimsical Moon may easily relate to Neptune's imaginative, dreamy nature, but when it comes to time and attachment, they're worlds apart. The Moon takes everything personally and is possessive. Neptune is unity and therefore selfless. The Moon and Neptune both come from the heart, connecting with what and who they love, but the Moon expects something in return. The Moon by nature is exclusive and conditional and Neptune is fully accepting of what is. Since true love does not have expectations, we might more accurately call the Moon's love affection. Neptune is the part of us capable of unconditional love. And the Moon, as the ego, is entirely built around its sense of self, apart from anything else. Neptune is indiscriminately inclusive. With Neptune, we're all part of the same energy field, sharing one mind. Nothing is mine or yours, not even our thoughts. It's all Ours.

We've been exploring the Moon as the emotional mind and keeper of memories. We know the Moon in each of us finds comfort in what it knows, which is dependent on the progression of history. In Jiddu Krishnamurti's last journal, *Krishnamurti to Himself* (a compilation of reflections recorded near the end of his life), he says: "The whole psyche is memory and nothing else." He also focuses on time being thought; time *is* thought.[14] We've already linked the Moon with memory and history, which is based in time. And time is what keeps us and everything separate, divided, and identifiable. The Moon, which we've also associated with the mind or emotional mind, holds and comforts us with time, which we're now considering as thoughts. And, of course, our Moon-mind is personally reacting to how those thoughts make us feel.

Neptune is beyond time, form, space, and definition. We tend to look at ourselves and life as made up of things, but from the Neptunian view, there is no thing; it's all interconnected. Krishnamurti says it so well: "If there is no continuity what is there? There is nothing. One is afraid to be nothing. Nothing means not a thing—nothing put together by thought, nothing put together by memory, remembrances, nothing that you can put into words and then measure. There is most certainly, definitely, an area where the past doesn't cast a shadow, where time, the past or future or present, has no meaning."[15] That area he speaks of is what we understand as Neptune.

SELFLESS AND INCLUSIVE NEPTUNE

Neptune in astrology is the planet of reality—the reality underneath everything our minds have convinced us is real. When it's strongly placed in a chart or activated by transit, it's time to expand into a greater state of consciousness. Neptune is what connects our ego-selves to the cosmic wholeness. It represents both the collective of which we are a part and how we experience that mysterious collective as an individual.

Similar to Uranus, it draws us into the unknown, and when faced with the unknown, we instinctively seek the familiar. It's hard for us humans to see anything but our thoughts and images. We create life from what we think we know and leave little room for it to arise just as it is. Even Neptune's discovery was initially hidden from the human mind, although it was seen in the sky. The official discovery date is 1846, but in 1612, Galileo saw Neptune and thought it was a star. Planets beyond Saturn hadn't been discovered at that time, so he wasn't even *thinking* about that … and missed it. Neptune can be like a haze or fog and Neptunian times can feel confusing or unclear. The whole point is to let go of the old ideas, labels, and beliefs that keep you trapped in illusions. If you stay through the fog with patience and are willing to surrender, it will clear, revealing crystal clarity.

Neptune corresponds with The Hanged Man Major Arcana XII tarot card. The number 12 represents the boundary of time—3 multiplied by 4 equals the divine (3) on the cross of matter (4). The Hanged Man calls for an ego sacrifice that allows you to discover and experience more of your true essence and the deeper meaning of life. On the card, he's pictured hanging upside down from a tree, bound by a foot to the branches and arms tied behind his back. In some decks, his facial features are blurry, showing his release of ego identification. The Norse god Odin is commonly depicted as The Hanged Man and it's a great Neptunian story. Per legend, Odin got caught in the World Tree and hung suspended between heaven and earth for nine nights. His ravens and horse couldn't free him, and he struggled with himself until he reached a state of surrender. When he did, he perceived the magical runes, known as the keys to the secrets of existence.

With Neptune, we're faced with what we can't control or explain. We might experience some type of loss. The dream turns into a nightmare, false illusions dissolve, or maybe we get sick, tired, or sad enough that we finally let go. Letting go creates spaciousness and that's when Neptunian vision becomes clear, opening us to new dimensions of possibility. Neptunian love, compassion, faith, inspiration, and cosmic connection are expansive. They need more space than our egos want to allow, so we're always making more room.

CYCLES OF THE MOON AND NEPTUNE

Neptune takes 165 years to orbit the Sun, almost at a standstill compared to fast-moving Moon with its 29.5-day cycle. Neptune spends almost 14 years in each sign. Just like Uranus, unless it's at its transition point, Neptune holds a steady position in the same sign while the Moon goes through many of its complete monthly cycles. The Moon meets Neptune on the same ground round after round, receiving that same Neptunian flavor for years. So right now, as we write this, we're all receiving an infusion of Neptune in Pisces every month when the Moon transits by aspect. And really, regardless of the aspects, just the fact that Neptune is in Pisces is a constant influence in all our personal lives. Our collective ego, mind, memory, heart—whatever you like to call it, is being called to move away from all the divisions we create and recognize we're in this together. We belong to each other, whether we like it or not. Our individual thoughts and actions affect us all. Neptune knows this and is making waves to help us all remember that universal rhythm.

BRIDGING TIME AND TIMELESSNESS

So how are we as human beings bridging time and timelessness? The key is in our hearts and beyond words. Words are rooted in the past, which always makes them suspect, especially with Neptune, but we'll still try to use some here. Accepting this and letting go of attachment to words and thoughts is a main part of the Moon-Neptune evolutionary bridge. We can look at this in different ways, one being the bridge between body and spirit. The phasal relationship between the Moon and Neptune is a window into the integration of time-bound human physicality and timeless Spirit or Essence. It's also the bridge between the micro and macrocosm.

We're each both the part and the whole; the one and the All; a thing and nothing.

We can look at the Moon as Chronos time and Neptune as Kairos time. Chronos time is linear or sequential and Kairos is time that stands still, sometimes called the divine or supreme moment. Moon-Neptune is also a bridge of the heart. When you discover something in your heart or know it in yourself, you can recognize that same thing in others. Your personal experience makes you able to support and help others. It gives you empathy, which leads to compassion. The Moon tugs at your heartstrings, and when your heart opens, you're in the Neptune zone. The heart of the Moon is a bridge to the heart of the universe, where the rhythm of the body unites with the rhythm of the cosmos.

MOON-NEPTUNE PHASES

NEW PHASE (0–45 DEGREES APART) AND THE NEW CONJUNCTION

As always, the new phase is the beginning of a new evolutionary cycle and the mortal and immortal aspects of self are coming together in a brand-new way. Neptune has a strong influence on the Moon being so close to it, and the proximity of Neptune has a tendency to feel like greater forces taking over. It's important for individuals in this phase to remember that these "greater forces" include them, and in fact, a greater part of themselves *is* attempting to take over. There's a spiritual or imaginative part of the self that needs more freedom to express and develop. Moon-Neptune new phase people won't necessarily be conscious of this impulse, but it's a powerful force that will be felt. If the individual is spiritually or mystically inclined, this can be an exciting awakening. If the individual is uncomfortable with the mysterious energy that comes with Neptune, they may seek to escape and numb its influences.

Neptune is a planet of feeling and it heightens physical, emotional, and psychic sensitivity. In the new phase, this feeling will be a new experience on some level and can feel foreign or trigger emotional responses that seem to come from nowhere. A Moon-Neptune new phase person, especially at the conjunction, is particularly sensitive to the environment. The individual has just stepped through the door into a new state of consciousness and will need time to adjust. We can look at this as a baby born into a whole new world. Sometimes when we start a new cycle, we don't even recognize we've made the shift. It's doubtful a newborn baby grasps the magnitude and potential in its birth. Regardless, Moon-Neptune new phase individuals are finding a new rhythm that connects them with something greater. It's possible for the Moon to fall under Neptune's spell, resulting in losing one's sense of time and touch with the world. When planets have some shared motives, they can act in collusion. In this case, if the ego is very resistant to change, it can use the Neptunian energy to avoid facing reality and live in a fantasy world or use spirituality as a way to bypass the human experience. While it can feel like Neptune pulls you out of yourself, it's really trying to bring you more deeply in. The entire universe is also within each of us and in this phase, more of the "as without" is trying to make itself known within.

CRESCENT PHASE (45–90 DEGREES APART)

The new state of consciousness is now spreading its roots. A shift has happened and now it gets real—meaning it's not just an experiment or metaphorical automobile test drive. The sense of separate self has been infiltrated with a greater sense of connection to all things. How the Moon-Neptune crescent phase person responds is entirely personal. As an example, let's say a person in this phase has a long-time pattern of believing they only need to look out for themselves and their family. It's not that they have ill will towards others, they just don't feel connected with strangers in a meaningful way and so they're not on their list of concerns. Now, this person's starting to feel differently. One night, they needed assistance and a stranger stopped to help them. Then, to their surprise, someone asked them to organize a food drive for the homeless. The division between this person and the world is getting blurry. It would be easy to turn down the food drive responsibility and not complicate their life with more work. Plus, it will surely open a floodgate of feelings if they get personally involved. But they're in a new dimension, and part of them knows they can't ever go back. This is crescent phase: encountering resistance, making the changes grow, and embodying the new energy.

Individuals in Moon-Neptune crescent phase can support themselves by remembering that the old always challenges the new and each time it does they have a new opportunity to respond. The integration of body and spirit is difficult to write about because it's a language all its own. In crescent phase, there's always a search for value, meaning, and purpose. In this context, it's finding value in this new way of bridging the self with all of creation. Everyone looks at this differently and beliefs vary but we all have a desire to belong. The Moon seeks to belong with family and personal emotional connections. Neptune seeks to belong with something greater than self that unites us all. The bridge between the two links the common person with the spiritually enlightened … and we are all both. In this phase, the individual experiences stress between the old and new ways of experiencing reality. What used to seem like clockwork is now like a grandfather clock that chimes off-the-hour and is just a nostalgic sound. It takes effort to fix the clock or get rid of it altogether, but that time machine is no longer suitable or reliable. It's time to build what supports the new dimension.

FIRST QUARTER PHASE (90–135 DEGREES APART)

As with all first quarter phases, it's all about the action. The bridging of time and timelessness of body and soul is not in a thinking phase, it's in a doing phase. Individuals in the Moon-Neptune first quarter phase tend to make decisions based on their feelings and run with them. It's not until the effects of their actions hit them in the face that they see a bigger picture. We get the image of a child here and that can be accurate. There's a youthful optimism and desire to be seen that reminds us of a ten-year-old with a leading role in a school musical. But we're trying to talk about the cycle of integrating the separate self with all that is, and it doesn't translate so easily. Basically, the individual in this phase is creating situations where they can test out their current state of consciousness. They need experiences to learn what works for them and the "what" here is their relationship between the distinct, ego-self and unified spiritual or cosmic self. If there's too much ego, it's like living a shell of oneself, and at the heart, there's a feeling of emptiness. If there's too much spirit or unity, the personal sense of purpose gets lost and it's easy to float around aimlessly.

If time is thought and thought is the past, linked with the Moon, and timelessness is always now, linked with Neptune, it's pretty easy to figure out where you are in the mix. If you're thinking about anything, you're in the Moon zone. If you're in a moment where time stops, like when you lose yourself in the music, you're in the Neptune zone. Moon-Neptune first quarter phase people will know where they are timewise by what they do. Their choice of actions leads them directly into the time-space they want to experience.

They won't know it until it happens, and when it happens, they might blame someone else for the outcome. Either way, they have lots of opportunities to make new choices and try new things that yield different results. They won't know how separate (one) or connected (All) they want to be until they're in the moment. While it can create some chaos, and even some collateral damage, rushing into things leaves less room for dishonesty or falseness. It's hard to fake it when you're caught by surprise. In some ways, individuals in this phase are testing themselves to see how their body / spirit costume holds up in the real show.

GIBBOUS PHASE (135–180 DEGREES APART)

The gibbous phase can evoke a feeling that all is not well. When it comes to the relationship between body and spirit, we all know how much pain, insecurity, grief, anger, and shame we humans can create. How many books, blogs, and podcasts are there dedicated to body, mind, and spirit wellness? It's a top "problem" and a top seller. We make it hard on ourselves, being so attached to our thinking and believing those thoughts are real. This thought reality is linked with the Moon, and Neptune is a thoughtless reality. Moon-Neptune gibbous phase people are trying to make the two work together better by using the mind. Because the tool being used is the mind, that's where the power lies. But we need to consider what "mind" we're talking about and what voice the individual is listening to. There are so many variables and it's personal, but we can say that in this phase there's a deep need to question oneself and self-improve. On some level, the individual knows they can do better and they look for ways to do this. This could mean literally studying or training the mind to release old patterns and open to a greater field of consciousness. Time is also under review, especially the personal understanding of what time is and isn't. And how to work with/in it most effectively. Through this personal analysis, the individual gains knowledge and experience that is directly applicable to those around them. They may have a critical eye, but their hearts are selfless and they're quick to help others.

We've used the word *overcoming* for gibbous phase and anything connected with Neptune also has a flavor of overcoming because we can't approach Neptune without overcoming the past. To be more present in the now, history has to fall away. From the all-knowing Neptune mind, we made all that history up anyway. It doesn't matter because it isn't real, but the Moon isn't going to give it all up—no way! And after all, giving it all up isn't the point, but in Moon-Neptune gibbous phase, something does have to give. Because Neptune is involved, it's almost always a false illusion, a product of our one-mindedness that's keeping us from receiving the all-encompassing love, compassion, and truth of which we are a part. Once the individual in this phase corrects just one mental misperception, they shift the balance and realign the entire world towards more wholeness. It may be a micro-shift, but it's a shift nonetheless and it makes a difference.

FULL PHASE (180–225 DEGREES APART) AND THE OPPOSITION

And the baby is born! Well, that's the easiest way to look at the full phase—as the birth of what's been growing. Upon full phase, we leave the waxing half of the cycle and enter the waning. At this point the inner drive to produce and perfect something changes to the desire to get the most from whatever we're working with. The Moon's personal heart and Neptune's universal heart have been dancing to the same song for a while now and they know their moves. Imagine them on the dance floor, far apart and facing each other. It's the first time they've given each other this much room and if they look up, they might actually see each other fully for the first time. This is the feeling of full phase: something you think you've known suddenly shows up in a new light, and it always reflects you. It's not really new, of course, but the way you're observing it is new, so it marks a new phase of awareness. The Moon-Neptune full phase is the dawn of objectivity in the cycle and the relationship between the body and spirit will now be obvious, if the individual wants to see.

All aspects and phases are about integration, but integration literally defines the full phase and the opposition. With its Libran flavor, full phase is about bridging opposites, and in this case, the opposites are the one and All. By this point, we've used lots of words to describe the Moon and Neptune, so let's consider them all as opposites. We can look at them as body and spirit, time and timelessness, thing and nothing, heart and Heart, love and Love, ego and spirit, thought and absence of thought, past and present, and once again, one and All.

The Moon-Neptune relationship is a bridge between the most inner, personal planet (luminary) and the outermost, impersonal planet. Together they represent our wholeness as human and spiritual beings. To be clear, it's impossible for us ever to be un-whole or separate, but that doesn't stop us from seeing it that way. Individuals in this phase may look at their body and spirit as separate parts, maybe even at odds or in competition with each other. Same with the one and the All or the timebound world versus the vast expanse of timelessness. Polarity enhances the experience of separation so we can appreciate the differences and extremes along with how they reflect and complement each other. At this culmination or peak in the cycle, we expect to see more consciousness, but individuals in this phase need the mirror and feedback of others to see themselves with more clarity. No one forces us to see. Even when it's right in front of us we can choose not to look at it, not really. This phase is about seeing what/who we truly are and deciding to do something with it.

DISSEMINATING PHASE (225–270 DEGREES APART)

Now we get down to business. Whatever perspective the individual has about their body-spirit connection, even if it's none at all, they're ready to tell you all about it. Individuals in Moon-Neptune disseminating phase can feel like they're quite knowledgeable about spiritual and emotional matters, even at a young age. It wouldn't be uncommon for them to be explaining a greater truth about life on the playground or counseling a playmate. There's also a conditioned quality to this phase which can present as individuals sharing knowledge that they themselves have outgrown. There's a combination of self-righteousness and authority that can arise in this phase, which can make them persuasive and equally offensive. What's happening in the bridging of one and All is a realization that the old perception or state of consciousness is now becoming restrictive and preventing growth. Even if that perception has worked out advantageously in the past, it will not support the future.

Disseminating phase individuals want to be valued, respected members of society. They feel they have wisdom to offer and are usually willing to work hard to earn their rightful place in the community. In the Moon-Neptune cycle, this phase is often expressed through some type of work that contributes to the physical and emotional care and/or spiritual development of everyday people. The Moon is now approaching Neptune again and the distance between them is less. We can imagine the Moon is on its way home and looking forward to returning to its origins. On its way, it will happily connect with others and bring them along. When individuals in this phase share their wisdom about the interconnectivity of the microcosm and macrocosm and the body and spirit, they're always having a conversation about "home." Home implies belonging and with Moon-Neptune, we can imagine, create, and embody the ultimate heart home; the ultimate sanctuary. Even if a Moon-Neptune disseminating phase person has no interest or belief in anything beyond a material, finite world, you'll find them trying somewhere or somehow to lead others to more security and safety.

LAST QUARTER PHASE (270–315 DEGREES APART)

Now the Moon has turned the corner into the last stretch before returning to Neptune. It won't be long before this whole cycle is complete, and the next leg of the journey begins. Just like towards the end of life, we often become aware of the most important things towards the end of a cycle. We say hindsight is 20/20 almost like it's too bad we didn't take a better look earlier, but that 20/20 vision came *through* the experience. We didn't have it before, period. During the Moon-Neptune last quarter phase, we often finally get the memo and awaken to things we'd suppressed or missed before. The realm of one and All and time and timeless is filled with the unknown. The Moon, protecting our psyche and sanity, limits how much unknown we're ready for and doesn't give us more than we can receive at the time. It also runs the same story, reactions, and associated emotions for as long as we need them. Individuals in the last quarter phase are ready to break through and liberate from some of that ego protection.

We know the keyword for the last quarter phase is *re-orientation* and applying that to Moon-Neptune we can see how the physical and emotional body is re-orienting to itself in a greater context.

This greater context includes something beyond the self because Neptune is always more. Individuals in this phase are becoming less conventional and more open to the mysteries of the body and soul connection and the concept of time and all its implications. The contained Moon and uncontained Neptune may challenge each other for the driver's seat, but in the waning period of the cycle, it's like the last kick in a fight you know is already over. The ship is not ever turning around. But before it hits the inevitable shore, the individual has time for final insights and even a 360-degree turnaround in how and what they think about themselves and life from a more inclusive perspective. Everything they've been through and where they are now can take on a new meaning if they experience a change of heart. And a change of heart can be the most successful outcome of all.

BALSAMIC PHASE (315–360 DEGREES APART) AND THE BALSAMIC CONJUNCTION

And finally, the personal Moon, holding all the individual's history, and giving rise to the emotion that makes them human, draws close to Neptune. The one approaches the All and soon they will be indistinguishable. It's as if the thing is dissolving into nothing. Moon-Neptune balsamic phase people will all feel the vastness of creation, whether they experience it as a divine presence, nature, or unexplainable meaninglessness. Their psyches are infused with the mystical and acknowledged or not, they feel it in their bones. Neptune fog is hovering over what once seemed so clear and real. It's all questionable now and even the body is flowing with a different current. This is like the Bardo—the liminal or transitional space between living and dying; ending and beginning. In this space the consciousness is less connected with the body, opening psychic channels and doors to other dimensions. Sometimes, we're afraid of endings and the space between. This phase can definitely trigger that fear, but it also renews hope and faith if we're open to what's beyond.

Our original title idea for this book was "Releasing the Moon," and at the end of the Moon-Neptune cycle, the self is metaphorically released from the illusion of separation. Biologically we're birthed through the Moon womb, but in death, we return to Neptune, the cosmic womb. Neptune represents the initial source from which we arise and always return. Moon-Neptune balsamic phase people are reaching an end because they're almost ready for something new. The importance of the ego is generally lessening, and individuals may find themselves losing time or simply not constrained by it anymore. The balsamic phase can be fuzzy as life comes in and out of focus—like a light going out that flickers off and on. It's time to let go and merge with that cosmic rhythm we mentioned earlier. While these individuals are ready to enter a new state of body/spirit integration and development, their current wisdom and experience are invaluable to those approaching that phase themselves. Just like an aging person gives advice to a young adult, the Moon-Neptune balsamic phase individual gives the best of what they are and have now for the good of those who follow. We can call it sacrifice but it's not quite the right word. To use Neptune language: since we're all one, sacrifice and generosity don't apply. It's our *responsibility* to take care of ourselves, which includes taking care of each other. And at the end of cycles, that includes a graceful, meaningful close before surrendering to be reborn.

TEN
The Moon and Pluto: Bridging Ego and Soul

Pluto demands we move and change. The Moon delights in staying home and staying the same. The ego and soul do their dance, taking turns in the lead. If we didn't mention it before, no phase is more evolved than another. That would be a very egoic view but not whole or complete. Evolution isn't a ladder, it's a spiral. Your Moon-Pluto cycle gives you some information about one little turn in the spiral you've set out to grow through. It helps get your conscious mind on board with your deeper intentions. It also helps you anticipate the nature of the challenges you've come here to confront. It does not reveal how well you'll navigate your soul's intentions or what will happen to you on your journey. You have to live it. With Pluto, when it gets uncomfortable, you know it's getting real. Pluto is only concerned with the bottom-line: Truth.

"There is no coming to consciousness without pain," is the common expression (sometimes attributed to Carl Jung). In the context of Moon-Pluto, temporary pain is the greatest sign of growth.

In this book, Pluto is the farthest we journey from the Sun, and it leads us into a realm of darkness in respect to what we actually know about the trans-Neptunian objects. Working with Pluto has become more common in modern astrology, but its significance is certainly considered questionable by many. Pluto is the foundation of evolutionary astrology and not used at all in traditional Vedic astrology. Our discussion of it here comes from an evolutionary astrology perspective, but the energy and experiences that Pluto represents—such as intensity, obsession, compulsion, and our deepest emotional and psychological attachments—apply to all of us. Regardless of how we believe Pluto should be used in astrological practice, we can each relate to its energy, consciously and/or unconsciously.

Evolutionary astrology looks to Pluto as the soul's path of evolution or desire for a greater experience of itself. Pluto's natal placement by sign and house reveals how, in most recent past lives, the soul has chosen to develop, grow, and realize itself as an incarnate being. This type of astrology is based on the belief that the soul is directing, at least in part, its own evolution and awakening; that there's a deeper will and desire beyond the ego-self. Pluto represents the essence of what we are and is eternally motivated to transform or eliminate anything in the way of our growth. In this way, it poses the greatest threat to the Moon. What we often call "the dark night of the soul" is more accurately "the dark night of the ego." The soul doesn't care if the experience is uncomfortable. Its aim is solely to grow, whatever it takes. The ego, of course, resists, causing all kinds of tension. Mark Jones describes this as a cat clinging to a scrap of wood in a rushing river. When a firefighter comes to rescue the cat, it fights off the firefighter because it thinks the wood it's got its claws into is the only way. And so, it scrambles to hold on to what's going down. If you're interested in learning more about this and Pluto, we recommend Mark's book, *Healing the Soul: Pluto, Uranus and the Lunar Nodes.*[16]

TRANSFORMATIONAL PLUTO

Pluto was discovered in 1930, at the Lowell Observatory in Flagstaff, Arizona. At the time, it was named the ninth planet; in 2006, however, it was demoted to a "dwarf planet" by the International Astronomical Union (IAC) because it didn't meet all the criteria for full-sized planets. Pluto is part of the Kuiper Belt, a huge region in space beyond Neptune, made up of icy trans-Neptunian bodies. Pluto was the first of these to be discovered, but astronomers estimate there are seventy thousand of them. Pluto is beyond Neptune in the solar system, but for 20 years of its 248-year orbit, it's closer to the Sun than Neptune. If we look at Neptune as the great, vast unconsciousness, Pluto crossing its boundary and coming closer to the Sun illustrates the awareness of what we identify as unconsciousness.

Timewise, the discovery of Pluto coincided with a rising of depth psychology and the exploration of the relationship between the conscious and unconscious mind. While the idea of an unconscious mind goes way back, it was Sigmund Freud who introduced and popularized it in the early twentieth century. It's fitting that Pluto was discovered during the time psychoanalyst and psychiatrist Carl Jung was developing and sharing his concepts on personality, archetypes, and the collective unconscious. Pluto, with its actual orbit crossing in and out of the Kuiper Belt, signifies the bridge between consciousness and unconsciousness, and our ability to bring the shadow into the light.

Pluto symbolizes transformation, and interestingly, astronomers say its face changes during its orbit. When Pluto gets closest to the Sun, its icy surface warms up, evaporating to form a gas. When it moves away from the Sun, the gasses cool, and the surface refreezes. This change in atmosphere is a metaphor for our own changing, from pure spirit into body, all the phases in between, and back out again. Working with Pluto in astrological practice takes us into our deepest ingrained habits and drills down to that thing we've been going for over and over again. It's where we get stuck and also where we can free ourselves by letting go of the past and surrendering to a death that leads to rebirth.

Pluto also shows how we use power, where we give it away, and what we feel has power over us. It's our personal underworld, where we bury and hide things. It's also where we confront the secrets of our past and our shadow. When we talk about facing our monsters, we're in Pluto land. What we often don't realize is that some of our greatest gifts are buried with all the things we don't want to see or own. The Pluto in each of us *does not* want things to stay the same. It wants more for us and to feel fully alive, which requires an intimate dance with death and pushing our limits. Our ego-selves love to feel in control, but Pluto experiences remind us that's not the case. We try to manipulate the outside world to feel better, fix the problem, or fill the void, but as prominent Astrologer Laura Nalbandian has told her students: "There is no external solution to an internal problem." Pluto demands we face ourselves, own it all, and grow into our next best version.

CYCLES OF THE MOON AND PLUTO

Pluto takes 248 years to orbit the Sun, practically motionless compared to the fast-moving Moon with its monthly cycle. Pluto spends almost 21 years in each sign. Just like Uranus and Neptune, unless it's at its transition point, Pluto holds a steady position in the same sign while the Moon goes through approximately 250 complete monthly cycles. Moon meets Pluto on the same ground round after round, absorbing that same Plutonian flavor for years. Pluto magnifies anything it contacts, and as we write this book, Pluto is in Capricorn, amplifying our current state of affairs socially, politically, environmentally, and economically. Basically, the world we've created has hit its maximum growth limits and stability and reliability are cracking.

Capricorn is known for keeping the ship going, but even with its remarkable focus and endurance, anything out of alignment will eventually collapse. Pluto is the agent of transformation and the Moon is the guardian of preservation. For our well-being and survival, we need to find a way to convince the Moon in ourselves, individually and collectively, that going down with the ship we know isn't the answer. Our hope is in learning to swim and navigating new waters. It's in choosing something different and adapting ourselves to what we need now. Pluto propels us from the core of our being and when we align with that true guidance or compass, we can overcome anything.

BRIDGING THE EGO AND SOUL

We've already said it, but it's worth repeating that letting go is a requirement for Pluto. While it involves letting go of the past, it's really a letting go *into* something new. Bridging the ego (Moon) and soul (Pluto) is about getting to the bottom line of what you need at this point in your journey of self-discovery. The Moon will have its near-sighted emotional reactions to Pluto. From the Moon's side, Pluto looks like the edge that drops into the abyss. The Moon, tied to the physical body, experiences sensations that are hard to ignore. It will do all it can to save itself from the fire of transformation. No matter how much moody, worried Moon objects, hides, cries, or digs its heels in, Pluto will not be stopped or swayed from its agenda. It sees things through an entirely different lens. Its laser-like vision penetrates the Moon's façade of reality and safety.

In his book, *The Soul's Desire and the Evolution of Identity: Pluto and the Lunar Nodes*, Adam Gainsburg writes: "A Soul is not bound by time and space. It views incarnational experience and manifest creation only as it can: from its perspective. It will see the possibilities of incarnational experience from its own state of wholeness, as infinitely varied shades of possibilities of light, love, sound or shape. It will not see the distinctions between the sign energies of astrology, for example, because it has no vibrational need of doing so. It will see their differences instead as a variegated unity."[17]

The Moon-Pluto cycle reveals where we're at with respect to integrating specific conscious and unconscious aspects of ourselves. We live consciously by the Moon, seeking familiar comforts, like a special person to love, a pet, the blanket Grandma made, and all the things we know and treasure. Living by the Moon, we identify ourselves by the personality or self-identity we've created, with its qualities, needs, and history. We also live by Pluto, desiring to follow the calling of our souls to know ourselves as the energy or undercurrent that flows through, but is not attached to any of it. Moon, though it's traditionally considered a night planet, is still a luminary and vessel of light. It seeks to illuminate through reflection. Pluto is the darkness and shadows, which inherently involves light, but it emphasizes where light is absent. The bridging of ego and soul, light and shadow, consciousness and unconsciousness both preserve and transform us at the same time. Pluto can't do its soul work without something personal to lose. The Moon can't lose anything that's real in the heart of the soul.

MOON-PLUTO PHASES

NEW PHASE (0–45 DEGREES APART) AND THE NEW CONJUNCTION

Pluto conjunct the Moon is one of the most emotionally taxing experiences of life and forces us to take on things we're not necessarily comfortable with, especially within ourselves. Individuals in Moon-Pluto new phase might end up associating with people who have deeply intense personalities. In fact, individuals who live through this phase, or are born with the configuration, are often extremely intense themselves. From an evolutionary standpoint, this phase can be therapeutic as it offers lessons in living life through ups and downs, especially in extreme situations. These lessons are a gift of opportunities to self-review and change whatever is necessary to lead a more empowered life, aligned with the soul's intentions for growth.

The psyche of individuals in Moon-Pluto new phase can be overrun by the amount and severity of events that take place in life, which will have a direct effect on their psychological state. There's no exaggeration here when it comes to this feeling because we're all naturally resistant to change, and we carry a very heavy heart when we have to face one. The problem in accepting any change in this phase is that it can trigger fear and dark feelings about the shape of life in the future. Uncertainty creeps in to haunt, which makes it difficult to reach any conclusion in terms of making decisions. New phase is a just-do-it phase and eventually, these individuals are left with no choice but to go through the drastic changes in life, especially from a psychological point of view.

The emotional attachments of Moon-Pluto new phase people will be primarily with their dear ones. Romantic relationships can be extremely intense and any break or betrayal in the relationship can significantly damage the spirit of these individuals, which may take a long time to heal. In another way, this phase is also about the self-healing process, which is the result of enduring pain through multiple transition points in life. The ego and soul are opposite spectrums of human experience and bridging the ego and soul is a very difficult practice to master. The Moon-Pluto new phase brings a fresh opportunity to do so.

CRESCENT PHASE (45–90 DEGREES APART)

As the Moon is now moving away from Pluto, it's able to visualize matters on its own and therefore, emotions run high but are much different from that of the new phase. This is because in Moon-Pluto crescent phase, individuals are more aware of what's happening around them, despite being emotional in most conditions. Moon-Pluto crescent phase people are good at dealing with others who are quite intense and hard to handle. They're also more prepared and ready to make some significant changes in the way they've been living.

In pursuit of spiritual experience, these individuals might part ways with those they feel may not be helpful in their future endeavors. They might give up ideologies they believe to be outdated. They're also likely to make quick and important changes to their living conditions, such as ending an important relationship, which will eventually lead to the beginning of another relationship and many new transformative experiences. While none of these are planned, the changes don't cease to occur, and the result is a complete period of quick transformations in the life of the individual.

While Moon-Pluto crescent phase people are quite ready to accept the changes they're initiating, they're also at the risk of losing enthusiasm if the change is not perceived as entirely positive, so they can be a bit cautious. While the ego (Moon) has more freedom away from the soul (Pluto), it gets acquainted with various experiences along the way and slowly detaches from the soul. As it separates, it becomes harder to see the whole truth. Most typical human beings expect to have comfort in whatever they choose, and when they don't find comfort, circumstances become difficult to accept. Pluto is a generational planet that offers experiences that force the individual into transformative challenges that will stay with them for many lifetimes to come.

FIRST QUARTER PHASE (90–135 DEGREES APART)

Moon-Pluto first quarter phase people can be extremely emotional, and it's not wise to play a prank on them because they can turn very serious when they take it personally. As the Moon progresses in its journey, it evolves with the experiences and mental perspective of the individual, who at this point can take themselves quite seriously and react emotionally. They might be going through some painful periods and experiencing emotional disturbance. This is yet another pivotal phase where the individual is eternally bound to make forceful changes to their psychological and physical environments.

In some ways, the Moon-Pluto first quarter phase is the correction-point for egocentric actions that occurred in the prior course of the individual's life path. The type of actions driven by the ego's selfishness that disrupted the evolution of the human mind in its highest sense. The ego wants everything it desires, but the soul doesn't demand anything. The soul is an essence that is unaltered yet has a solid focus on the truth and righteousness. This is a phase where individuals might have to eliminate some of their obsessions and accept the turning point in life that will eventually align them with their greater purpose.

The trust factor is very important during this phase and these individuals will trust people once they become acquainted with them at a reasonably deeper level. This is because they don't have much time to analyze a person to see if they would be an integral part of their existence along with that of the cosmos or universe. Troubled or failed relationships are a huge burden to carry during this phase and just seem to add salt to the wound. It's important to stay focused on their own path instead of looking at others, so the individual doesn't create another disruption in the process of bridging ego and soul.

In the Moon-Pluto first quarter phase, there's a tendency to seek applause and attention, which distorts the genuine expression of self. Competition and showmanship can turn empty. Jealousy can ruin the beauty of innocence. Yet through it all, this phase has the potential for unparalleled creative actualization.

GIBBOUS PHASE (135–180 DEGREES APART)

Moon-Pluto gibbous phase individuals have been accepting life as it comes, with or without liking it, and life presents more options than before for those in this phase. These individuals are usually more confident and clear in their approach to life. This naturally puts them in a better state of mind to deal with challenging situations. They also maintain a stable mind in emotionally tense circumstances as they've already experienced such emotional intensity and are better equipped to handle it. The ego tackles the conditions of life very well to stay in line with the soul's purpose.

These individuals have good instincts about various emotional situations in life and can easily act, considering the possible outcomes in their minds. Having said all this, these individuals are certainly not overconfident, and if their level of consciousness supports it, they are constantly on the lookout for the greater purpose of the soul. In most cases, not even the most dramatic events jolt their presence of mind because their emotional brain is well intact with an understanding of reality and many of the other hidden realms where Pluto takes the ego. This doesn't mean these individuals can't be emotionally challenged. It just means they're in a better position to handle such hardcore challenges.

Moon-Pluto gibbous phase people, apart from handling crises well in their own lives, are also capable of being excellent counselors to those who are reeling due to emotional trauma. They have this adept ability to get deep into the psychological realms of a human being with more considerable ease than others. This allows them to be helpful in many emotionally tricky and troublesome situations.

FULL PHASE (180–225 DEGREES APART) AND THE OPPOSITION

With the ego (Moon) and soul (Pluto) opposing each other, individuals will have a lifetime experience of bridging soul and ego at various junctures in this incarnation. They have an innate sense of differentiation and harmony between ego and soul that helps them achieve both personal and spiritual success. Moon-Pluto full phase people have the capability of understanding the need to balance both material and spiritual life. It's difficult for these individuals to get emotionally connected to someone from the get-go because it's easier for them to stay detached in their pursuit of this spiritual experience.

The constant need to take care of themselves is a most prominent matter in the lives of these individuals. They have to communicate with their inner spirit to understand the deeper meaning of life. Rather than finding inspiration outside, these individuals are very good at finding it from their inner self and past experiences. And they can make the best use of their life experiences in their process of evolution. Since full phase is always about relationships, it's equally important for Moon-Pluto full phase individuals to share their inspiration and collaborate with others.

Moon-Pluto full phase is an emotional transformation where individuals must transcend the deepest inner horizons beyond the mere material pursuits of their lives. They're gaining awareness and understanding of the actual purpose of life to be a perennial student of learning—learning the art of studying the profound wisdom in the process of their evolution as a human being. Due to the opposition and its inherent tug-of-war, these individuals always need to distinguish between the never-ending wants of the human emotional mind and the desire of the inner spiritual being—the soul.

DISSEMINATING PHASE (225–270 DEGREES APART)

The Moon has more say in this phase with Pluto, and emotions run high when the individual feels the need to be under the guidance of someone wise. The very nature of the Moon-Pluto combination is serious and intense, and this phase reflects that, especially in terms of handling romantic relationships. Deep and intense thoughts and feelings for loved ones might just increase to higher levels and the feeling of intimacy is enhanced.

On the other hand, the Moon-Pluto disseminating phase also indicates creativity of the darker side—and we don't mean "dark" in any negative sense but of the shadows. These individuals can surprise the community with their creative and artistic energy in a very unexpected manner. One who appears to be a "bad-ass" might surprisingly have a creative quotient working to the best of its potential from behind the scenes. As the Moon is powering its way through, these people can express themselves to the general public in a very intense manner. Their intuitive powers and presence of mind can be good but at the same time can turn out to be controversial. It's important for these individuals to be mindful of what they say to people beyond their close circles.

The creative energies of Moon-Pluto disseminating phase individuals can influence a larger community and its progress expansively, subject to the nature of the entirety of the birth chart. If the energy of Pluto is directed constructively, these people can portray a powerful display of their creative and artistic skills to the public, being a significant motivational influence. These individuals have the ability to storm into the hearts of others.

LAST QUARTER PHASE (270–315 DEGREES APART)

This is another phase that imposes multiple changes to the psychological and physical environments of the individual. Some events from the past will continue to remain as a lasting memory, which will intensify the mindset of these individuals, and they are pretty serious about their emotional and psychological needs. These people can be obsessed with their emotional attachments, making it extremely difficult for them to go through any changes—but at times, change is the only option. Since Moon-Pluto last quarter phase individuals are often not ready for any more change, especially from a psychological point of view, the transition from their conditioned existence to make room for something new can be emotionally painful and challenging. They may need to separate from the people and belongings they've been emotionally attached to, and even more so, from their entire sense of self-identity.

During the Moon-Pluto last quarter phase, it becomes increasingly difficult for individuals to develop new bonds with people who become part of their lives in some manner. This refraining attitude can make them appear cold or insensitive, leaving them vulnerable to being misunderstood. However, individuals in this phase are battling the most intense emotional barriers from within to get settled with whatever they have to face at a particular point of time, in terms of emotional safety and stability.

Although this is a critical phase in the evolutionary development of the human mind to come in line with the philosophical idea of acceptance, the transitional phase from one emotional part or level of life to another is a painful experience altogether. It's important for individuals in this phase to release their self-destructive habits and behaviors to help themselves transform into a more conscious and liberated state of being.

BALSAMIC PHASE (315–360 DEGREES APART) AND THE BALSAMIC CONJUNCTION

The Moon-Pluto balsamic phase is one of the most, if not the most, intense phases of human life. It's important not to consider this phase as a negative one and to notice the silver lining in the dark circle that we're surrounded with, staying calm and composed. There's always hope, and we only know light in contrast to the dark. During this phase of potential distress, with less external guidance and a decayed belief system, we're left to face darkness and dissatisfaction. At the deepest level, individuals in this phase may feel a loss of protection, as they're out of their own conscious sight.

We can see the beauty of darkness only in the dark. We can feel the bliss of blindness only if our eyes are absent of sight. This is where and when we're exposed to some of the most mystical ideas that bring up revolutionary changes to our lives and ideologies of existence. Individuals in this phase are exposed to the more occult and mysterious sides of life and can develop a great balance between the mundane and mystical. It's important to remain receptive and even submissive to nature during this phase. Secrets are being revealed. Moon-Pluto balsamic phase people need to experience the energy of what's brewing in and around them because they won't have a clear vision of what's happening or real.

Surreal things happen and new ends meet at various unexpected times in life. This is the end before the beginning of the confluence of ego and soul and that's a seriously encouraging thought. We learn how to solve and resolve the issues of the past during this phase and get ready to move on in our journeys as and when we're gradually able to visualize the actual realities of life.

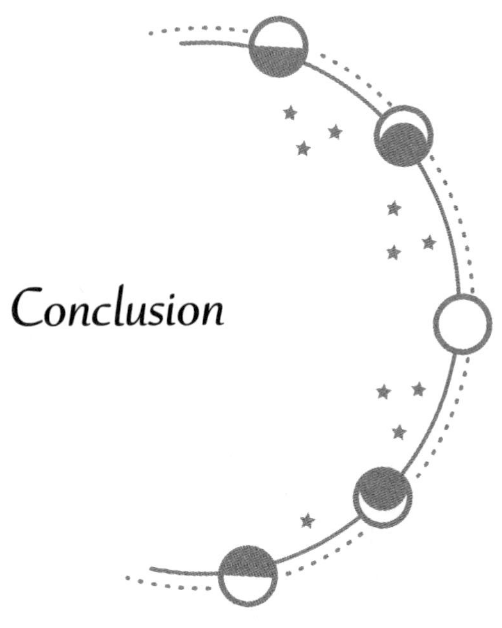

Conclusion

With the Moon, we can analyze the inner self and the psychological well-being of an individual. The Moon's association with signs, houses, planets, and aspects reveals the dynamics of the state of human well-being. Throughout this book, we aimed to provide deep insight into how to bridge our ego, or innermost personal self (represented by the Moon), with different aspects of ourselves, including those less personal (represented by the other planets). A big part of our journey of self-discovery is understanding what we're up to now and how we can equip ourselves for what we're headed to face in the future. This gives us some clarity, and clarity results in a freer mind with better vision. It helps us see more clearly where we are, what we're doing, why we're doing it, and what lies ahead.

Just like any other practice, astrology is something we get better at as we keep doing it. Reflecting on and writing about our experiences, and talking with others who shared their experiences, made writing this book a personal transformational process for us. Much of the time, we see what we want to see and fail to see what astrology, or life, is actually showing us. When it comes to astrology, we usually default to what we've learned and leave it at that. Looking at something in a new way or trying a new technique opens a doorway to something different. When you don't know the answer or interpretation, you make room for the cosmos to speak directly to and through you. In creating this material, we did our best to listen to the Moon and all the planets. To understand the intricate experiences and growth that occur inside us as we live through the cycles of the Moon with respect to the other planets is a bit complicated, but it's a great treasure to uncover as it leads us into the very heart of the journey of self-discovery.

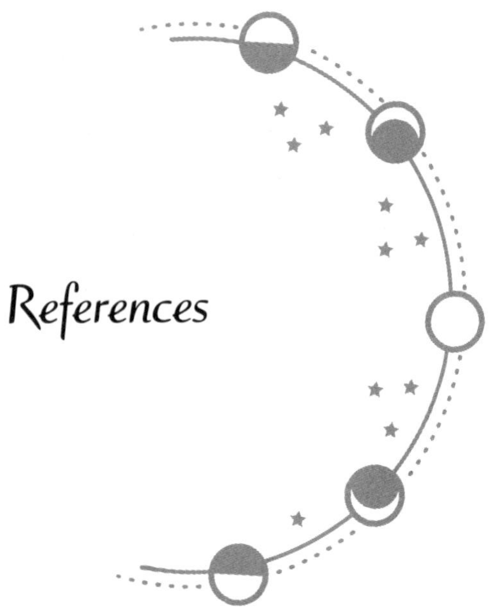

References

1. Richard Tarnas, *Cosmos and Psyche: Intimations of a New World View*, New York: Penguin Group, 2006, p. 109 (Personal Transit Cycles).

2. Chris Brennan, "Robert Hand on Reconciling Traditional and Modern Astrology," *The Astrology Podcast*, episode 12. Robert Hand spoke about his opinion of transits in astrology, which made so much sense to us. Transits are not always felt at an external level and most of the time, we feel them internally. This is probably true for every transit in the sky.

3. Dane Rudhyar, *The Lunation Cycle: A Key to the Understanding of Personality*, Santa Fe, NM: Aurora Press, 1967. This is an emphasis on what Rudhyar explains through his work.

4. Three Initiates, *The Kybalion*, CreateSpace independent publishing platform (rough draft printing), 2012, p. 16. This is just one of many books about Hermetic philosophy and principles, based on the teachings of Hermes Trismegistus. This specific reference is to the Law of Correspondence.

5. Gregg Henriques, "What Is the Mind?" Psychology Today. December 22, 2011. https://www.psychologytoday.com/ie/blog/theory-knowledge/201112/what-is-the-mind. Accessed May 2021.

6. This quote attributed to the French philosopher René Descartes turned out to be a powerful philosophical statement because human beings have been what they thought or think, and that fundamental idea has never changed. Our presence of mind is largely driven by what we think. What we think is what we are under any given situation.

7. Dale Carnegie, *How to Win Friends and Influence People*, New York: Simon and Schuster, 1936, p. 14.

8. This quote is from *Serious Creativity: Using the Power of Lateral Thinking to Create New Ideas*, New York: Harperbusiness, 1993. www.debono.com/quotes-1. Accessed May 2021.

9. Marcus Aurelius, *Meditations*, a translation by George Long, Fingerprint Classics, 2017, book VI, p. 94.

10. Robert Wilkinson, *Saturn: Spiritual Master, Spiritual Friend*, Kindle Edition, Fifth Ray Publishing, 2017, p. 10.

11. Dane Rudhyar, *The Astrology of Personality: A Re-Formulation of Astrological Concepts and Ideals, in Terms of Contemporary Psychology and Philosophy*, New York: Doubleday Paperback Edition, 1970, p. 258.

12. American astrologer and lecturer Steven Forrest has published many books, and among our favorites are *The Elements Series (The Book of Fire, The Book of Earth, The Book of Air, The Book of Water)* and *The Book of Neptune.* This reference is not to a specific quote but a remembrance of his wisdom through his works.

13. Jeffrey Wolf Green, *Uranus—Freedom from the Known*, School of Evolutionary Astrology, 2014, p. xiii.

14. Jiddu Krishnamurti, *Krishnamurti to Himself,* Harper One, 1987, p. 66.

15. Ibid., p. 67.

16. Mark Jones, *Healing the Soul: Pluto, Uranus and the Lunar Nodes*, Raven Dreams Press, 2011.

17. Adam Gainsburg, *The Soul's Desire and the Evolution of Identity: Pluto and the Lunar Nodes*, Soulsign, 2006, p. 2.

Bibliography

BOOKS

Forrest, Steven. *The Book of Neptune*. Borrego Springs, CA: Seven Paws Press, 2016.

———. *The Inner Sky: How to Make Wiser Choices for a More Fulfilling Life*. Borrego Springs, CA: Seven Paws Press, 2012.

Gainsburg, Adam. *Sacred Marriage Astrology: The Soul's Desire for Wholeness*. Nashville, TN: Cold Tree Press, 2005.

———. *The Soul's Desire and the Evolution of Identity: Pluto and the Lunar Nodes*. Soulsign Publishing, 2006.

Green, Jeffrey Wolf. *Uranus—Freedom from the Known*. School of Evolutionary Astrology, 2014.

Henriques, Gregg. *A New Unified Theory of Psychology*. Springer, 2011.

Jones, Mark. *Healing the Soul: Pluto, Uranus and the Lunar Nodes*. Portland, OR: Raven Dreams Press, 2011.

Jung, Carl. *Synchronicity: An Acausal Connecting Principle*. Routledge, 1985.

Krishnamurti, Jiddu. *Krishnamurti to Himself.* Harper One, 1987.

Rudhyar, Dane. *The Astrology of Personality: A Re-Formulation of Astrological Concepts and Ideals, in Terms of Contemporary Psychology and Philosophy*. Doubleday Paperback Edition, 1970.

———. *The Lunation Cycle: A Key to the Understanding of Personality*. Santa Fe, NM: Aurora Press, 1967.

Tarnas, Richard. *Cosmos and Psyche: Intimations of a New World View*. New York: Penguin Group, 2006.

Three Initiates. *The Kybalion*. CreateSpace independent publishing platform (rough draft printing), 2012.

Wilkinson, Robert. *Saturn: Spiritual Master, Spiritual Friend*. Kindle Edition, Fifth Ray Publishing, 2017.

PODCAST

Brennan, Chris, "Robert Hand on Reconciling Traditional and Modern Astrology," *The Astrology Podcast*.

WEBSITES

Cafeastrology.com/calendars/moonphasescalendar: information on general moon phases

Cafeastrology.com/whats-my-moon-sign: Look up your moon sign and learn more about it. Also has general information about moon phases.

Tarot.com/astrology/moon-phases: information on general moon phases

TO WRITE TO THE AUTHOR

If you wish to contact the author or would like more information about this book, please write to the author in care of Llewellyn Worldwide Ltd. and we will forward your request. Both the author and publisher appreciate hearing from you and learning of your enjoyment of this book and how it has helped you. Llewellyn Worldwide Ltd. cannot guarantee that every letter written to the author can be answered, but all will be forwarded. Please write to:

Tara Aal
Aswin Subramanyan
℅ Llewellyn Worldwide
2143 Wooddale Drive
Woodbury, MN 55125-2989

Please enclose a self-addressed stamped envelope for reply, or $1.00 to cover costs. If outside the U.S.A., enclose an international postal reply coupon.

Many of Llewellyn's authors have websites with additional information and resources. For more information, please visit our website at http://www.llewellyn.com.